SELF GOVERNMENT FOR INDIA

SELF GOVERNMENT FOR INDIA

UNDER THE BRITISH FLAG

V. S. SRINIVASA SASTRI

GYAN

Published by

Gyan Publishing House
5, Ansari Road
Daryaganj, New Delhi-110002
Phone: 011-47034999, 9811692060
E-mail: books@gyanbooks.com

Distribution Network
gyanbooks.com
India, USA, Canada, UK, Australia

ISBN: 978-93-7225-102-9 (PB)

First Published, 1916

2nd Impression 2025

Printed at: Gyan Press, Delhi.

SELF GOVERNMENT FOR INDIA

Author: V. S. SRINIVASA SASTRI

SELF-GOVERNMENT FOR INDIA

UNDER THE BRITISH FLAG

BY

V. S. SRINIVASA SASTRI

Servants of India Society

ALLAHABAD

1916

Eight Annas

This pamphlet, crude and with many shortcomings, is laid at the feet of the Mother as a loving and reverent offering. Maybe it will help in making her cause better understood and leading her sons to think more earnestly of it.

The quotations may weary and distract the advanced reader, but there are many who, at every step of unfamiliar ground, would like their judgment fortified by the authority of great names.

Servants of India Home, *Poona,* *20th December 1916.*	V. S. Srinivasa Sastri.

SELF-GOVERNMENT FOR INDIA

UNDER THE BRITISH FLAG

INDIA'S CLAIM

THE OCCASION

In April 1855, with much misgiving and amid the gloomy forebodings of his countrymen, Cavour sent an army of 15,000 men to aid France and England in the Crimean war. It was a great risk for the little State of Piedmont, but a creditable compaign would bring it a place among the great nations of Europe. Luckily, the army distinguished itself for gallantry and discipline. When next year Cavour visited Paris, Louis Napoleon asked him the fateful question, "What can be done for Italy?" And at the Conference of Paris, notwithstanding the opposition of Austria, Italy was admitted on equal terms with the other Powers and her wrongs secured a hearing from them. A similar stroke of genius was performed by Lord Hardinge when he despatched an Indian expeditionary force to the fields of Flanders within a few weeks of the outbreak of the gigantic war of to-day. The gallant Indian army has not only covered itself with distinction, but won for India a position in the British Empire which decades of diplomacy and agitation could not have won. English statesmen vied with one another in acknowledging the "spontaneous" and splendid rally of India to the Empire. At a great meeting in Guildhall in May last the Prime Minister, after recounting the gifts and offers of the princes and noblemen of India, referred to the deeds of the Indian army and said: "Then again "when we look to the actual achievements of the "forces so spontaneously despatched, so liberally provided, so magnificently equipped, the battlefields of "France and Flanders bear undying tribute to their "bravery and devotion." Mr. Bonar Law, who followed, avowed his belief that as a nation the British had more reason to be proud of the spontaneous enthusiasm on behalf of their Emperor and the Empire of the Indian princes and peoples than they had to be proud of the conquest of India. The Marquess of Crewe on the same occasion struck a higher note: "He for his part would like also to think that the "association of India and of the Colonies at such a "gathering as that was a significant sign of the essential comprehension which, as the years rolled on, "would, he fully believed, sweep away all these "obstacles of distance, of creed, or of race which "seemed to interfere with the complete union of the "different members of the great Imperial Confederation—a union which would hinge upon the free "activities of each and which would be finally "based upon a common belief in the progress of "the whole." "The changed angle of vision" of Mr. Charles Roberts has become the current coin of Indian political parlance. Lord Hardinge himself, looking forward to the future of India, used a phrase which has become classical. India would be a "true friend of the Empire, not a trusty dependant." Most politicians must have eagerly asked him, "What can be done for India?" In the first outburst of wonderment and gratitude, leaders of opinion in England, heedless of Anglo-India, expressed a clear desire to accord to India a political status more or less of equality with her sister nations.

Expectation in India was raised to the highest pitch. By common consent Government and subjects alike refrained from controversy of every kind, not merely to impress on the enemy the strength of the Imperial sentiment in this country, but as a symbol of the new spirit of perfect concord and unity of purpose. This unwillingness to disturb the general harmony was nowhere more manifest than in the subdued tone adopted by Indian leaders in urging their claims to a great constitutional advance in the near future. In the select circle of politicians who initiate ideas and movements, there went round one of those whispers which arise from an unknown source, but which gain credence none the less on that account, to the effect that a great scheme of reform was in process of formulation, to be announced as a free and voluntary gift from a grateful empire to a faithful people, and that nothing was to be done by the latter which might mar the spontaneity and grace of the gift. The spell, however, was soon broken. India figured less and less in the plans of reconstruction that the great organs of public opinion in England put forward now and again, and Ministers of State began to observe in references to this country a caution and restraint in glaring contrast with the exuberance of their earlier utterances, as though they had been admonished of their imprudence by the gathering forces of reaction.

The self-governing Colonies, or as they now like to style themselves, the Dominions, have advanced a claim to a voice in the determination of questions of peace and war and, as a natural consequence, undertaken to bear a share of the cost of Imperial defence. The claim has met with an encouraging reception from responsible authorities in the United Kingdom. The preoccupations of the hour preclude an immediate settlement of such issues, but it appears likely that desire for closer union among the different parts of the empire will lead to the establishment of a new Imperial Parliament with an executive subordinate to it, in which the United Kingdom and the oversea Dominions will be represented. The place of India in this large scheme is a question that cannot fail to strike the minds of politicians who discuss the subject with any seriousness. It gets, however, a disproportionately small share of their attention. No wonder the public mind of the country is in a state of sore uneasiness. If the leaders of Indian opinion remained silent any longer, the impression might gain ground abroad that India would remain content with her present position in the Empire or with such slight constitutional advance as British statesmen in their generosity might offer.

Within the last few months the voice of the people has become audible. They have manifested an ambition for a place of honour in the new scheme of empire. This ambition will find embodiment in a scheme of self-government adopted at the coming sessions of the Indian National Congress and the All-India Muslim League. It is expected further that these political organisations will appoint delegates from different provinces, who should proceed to England and press the scheme on the attention of the Ministers of State and other leading statesmen. The Premiers of the Dominions are in constant and intimate touch with the Cabinet of the day, which includes the front men of all parties, and without a doubt they are using the countless opportunities of private and semi-official negotiation that they enjoy for preparing the ground so that, as soon as the moment is ripe, they can get their proposals under way for formal consideration. The champions of India labour already under a great disadvantage in this respect and her hopes, never so high as at this juncture, run a serious risk of being wrecked by any avoidable delay in the presentment of her case at the bar of English pubic opinion.

THE IMPERIAL CONFERENCE

It has been suggested that the Imperial Conference which will meet in the early part of next year should take the initiative in calling together a Convention of delegates from the United Kingdom and from the Dominions for making definite proposals of Imperial reconstruction after the war. Into the Imperial Conference India has claimed entry. In accepting the resolution on this subject in the Viceroy's Legislative Council, Lord Hardinge left it in doubt whether India will obtain admittance at all, because in his opinion the matter must be decided by the Conference itself. This, however, is perhaps an erroneous opinion. Prof. Keith, discussing this very question in his *Imperial Unity and the Dominions*, says: "It is quite impossible to accept "the validity of the argument of Lord Elgin in 1906 "that the constitution of the Conference cannot "be changed save by a resolution of the Conference. It can, it is clear, be changed by agreement "between the Imperial and the Dominion Governments "and such agreement should be secured forthwith." In fact this Conference has been called a Conference between Governments and Governments; and it would be a pity if India's representatives should wait to be summoned after the Conference had met.

Lord Hardinge was inclined to think that India should be represented by the Secretary of State and by an official delegate of the Government of India. A somewhat more liberal proposal is made by Mr. Basil Worsfold in a book recently published under the name of *The Empire on the Anvil.* According to this, besides the Secretary of State the Government of India should send two representatives, one elected by the official members and the other by the non-official members of the Legislative Council. It is possible to expect too much from our admission to this Imperial Conference. The fate of India will probably be decided by other bodies. In any case we cannot afford to let judgment go by default.

THE DANGER AHEAD

The Dominion representatives argue that if the foreign relations of the federated Empire were to be determined by the representatives of the United Kingdom and of the Dominions sitting together in one Imperial Parliament, it follows as a corollary that this Parliament should likewise control the government of India, the Crown Colonies and other British possessions; for, in their judgment the people of India cannot be admitted as their equals to the Imperial Parliament. In future then, if this idea is to prevail, India will be under the government not of Great Britain, but of Great Britain and the Dominions conjointly. It seems, however, to be realised that there will be great objection to this change both in India and in Egypt. Nothing is said of the causes of the objection and no idea seems to be entertained of removing these causes. But the responsibility of ruling India will be accepted, Mr. L. Curtis assures us, as a high spiritual task, *viz.*, that of "preparing for feedom the races which cannot as yet govern themselves." To Mr. Richard Jebb, author of the book entitled, *The Britannic Question*, the task appears "one in which it is desirable that the "Britannic peoples should take an intelligent interest "and a common pride, because it would tend to elevate "the type of citizenship in their own countries by fostering the sense of a high public responsibility." This is the new humiliation that stares us in the face, if we do not make it clear betimes that we will not tolerate the pretensions of the Dominions to a share in the government of our country without our being admitted to an equally effective share in the government of the rest of the Empire. While the blood of Indian soldiers is mingling with the blood of Dominion soldiers in battlefields all over the world, it is not right, if one can help it, to stir up animosities. But patience is a difficult virtue to exercise when a certain set of people brand you as an inferior race, exclude you ruthlessly from their territory and then coolly offer to administer your affairs and exploit your resources, adding at the same time that it is all for the purpose of teaching you how to govern yourselves. A school of Dominion thinkers would indeed go so far as to say that the tutelage of India can have no end. Mr. Jebb expounds this kindly view: "Into that Britannic Union India has not the "potentiality of entering. . . . With their own immemorial civilizations, traditions and indigenous ideals "all essentially non-European and with their widely "different standard of living, all of which differentiate "the Indian peoples from the Britannic, a free exchange of population is not easy to contemplate. "The Asiatic-exclusion policy of the North American,

"Australasian and South African democracies is not "based on any evanescent fallacy. . . . The Britannic "States would require therefore to retain control, "supported by military force, of the foreign relation "of India for as long a future as can be foreseen at "present." This writer is not deterred from pushing his ideas to their full conclusion by any threat of retaliation on the part of India. The assurance of the following remarks is only equalled by their falsity: "In practice, however, there would be little like-"lihood of any merely retaliatory policy on the part "of India. The economic fact is that Europeans are "welcome not only as visitors but also as residents in "Asiatic countries, for the sake of the money they "bring in and the lead they can give in commercial "organization; whereas Asiatic residents, who are "generally drawn from a lower class of their native "society, are unwelcome to 'European' communities "owing to the money they take out and the impedi-"ment of their cheap labour to the progressive ad-"vance of industrial and social standards, let alone "the impossibility of assimilating them to western "democracy."

ADVICE TO DOMINIONS

These irritating quotations have been made to show how real is the apprehension that a policy of silence and easy trustfulness on our part will end in the tightening of our fetters and our having to serve more masters and worse masters. Will the Dominions pause in their pride and listen to the words of a wise monitor? "The Dominions cannot expect to share in "the position formerly enjoyed without question by "the United Kingdom, as the autocratic, if benevo-"lent, controller of the destinies of the country. The

" self-consciousness of the people of India, as voiced
" by the inheritors of English political aspirations,
" would decline to accept the theory that Indian
" policy could be controlled in any way by the
" representatives of the Dominions, and this refusal
" would be completely justified, in view of the fact
" that the Dominions shut their doors on the admission
" of Indians, and accordingly treat Indians as such
" as inferiors, on ground of race alone." "It follows
" inevitably that the Dominions cannot expect to
" be allowed to determine the destinies of the Empire
" of India, and from the point of view of the
" Imperial Government it is clear that in their general
" foreign policy they must expect to have in future to
" consider the views of India with as much care as
" they consider those of the self-governing Dominions.
" Their duty in either case is identical, and must be
" carried out without favour to either. It is inevitable,
" therefore, India should be allowed a voice in the
" Imperial Conference just as any self-governing Domi-
" nion is allowed : it is indeed ludicrous to think that
" New Zealand, South Africa, and Newfoundland are
" to be ranked as superior to this Empire of India : it
" is right further that that voice should be uttered by
" a representative of India other than the Secretary of
" State for India, preferably by a member of the Indian
" race. If the Dominion Governments recognize frank-
" ly and willingly this position, a great step in the
" effective consolidation of the Empire in sympathy
" will have been gained, and there is no matter in
" which more easy and obvious progress towards Im-
" perial unity could be made, and that, too, without
" any formality or difficulty. The services rendered by
" India in the war offer an unparalleled opportunity

"for such recognition." Dr. Keith, from whose book, *Imperial Unity and the Dominions*, the above passages are taken, is not content with warning the Dominions against self-conceit and aggression ; he points out the error of their former ways and bids them tread the path of justice and brotherliness. He says: "It is an essential condition for the attainment of "Imperial unity that the Governments of the Domi-"nions should take into their earnest consideration "the means by which, while preserving essential "homogeneity of race, free and unrestricted entry into "their territories shall be secured to all educated Bri-"tish Indian subjects, and that all restrictions which "are at present, on grounds of race or colour only, im-"posed on British Indians who are legitimately resid-"ent in the self-governing Dominions should be "rescinded."

THE DEMAND

Whether a federation of Greater Britain on the lines proposed by enthusiasts in and out of England be practicable and, if so, what should be its principal features are questions of high Imperial policy which need not be considered here. Our present concern is to protest against any arrangements which will leave us in a worse condition politically than we now are in and consign us to the position of a household drudge in the Imperial family, compelled to put on the livery not only of Great Britain but of New Zealand, Australia, South Africa, Canada, and petty Newfoundland. We look to the statesmen of Great Britain to defend our interests and our honour. Our only shield is the attainment of self-government under the British flag. Once mistress of her own destinies, India will know how to hold her own among the nations that owe allegiance to the British Crown. Her people cannot be reconciled to the continuance of the British connection unless their country, the greatest dependency of England, the brightest jewel in her diadem, be elevated to the status and privileges of a self-governing Dominion. This elevation should be accomplished or at least promised definitely before the edifice of the renovated Empire is completed. For during the negotiations that lead up to the reconstruction India should be represented by her own natural leaders, who cannot stand up for her as the representatives of the Dominions will stand up for them, unless like these they command the weight and prestige of an autonomous population behind them.

SOME COMPARISONS

THE COLONIES

The demand of Indians to be allowed to govern themselves is countered by the assertion that they are unfit for so high a task. It is alleged that when the English colonies were granted responsible government they had reached a higher standard of fitness than we have now attained. This is not historically true. The present prosperity and enterprise of the Dominions should be entirely forgotten when we try to picture the colonies as they were in the forties and fifties of the last century. Fifty years of political and economic independence, as the example of Japan shows us, can make wonderful changes in the condition of a people. Let it also be remembered that fifty years of the modern time are really much longer than the like period in any former century. Canada was the first of British colonies to be made self-governing, and it is in Canada that British political institutions are believed to have shown their happiest results. Luckily, we possess in the report of Lord Durham a graphic and in general a faithful description of the condition of the colony and its people at the time when the concession of responsible government was made. Canada was divided into two provinces, Lower and Upper Canada. In Lower Canada the population was 600,000, being divided into French 450,000 and English 150,000. Upper Canada had 400,000, mostly English. In both provinces there were representative institutions wholly elected with power of voting supplies and imposing taxes. But the Executive were appointed wholly by the Crown, and as they had control of certain revenues and other sources, were enabled to defy the legislature. The public offices were filled by men belonging to certain families, giving rise in Upper Canada to what was known under the odious name of the 'Family Compact.' There were bitter disputes arising out of the unjust way in which the Crown lands were distributed as well as what were known as the 'Clergy Reserves.' In Lower Canada the minority of the English practically monopolised political power and the public service, and the bulk of the trade was in their hands. The wrangles between the legislature and the Government were protracted and often led to violent recriminations. In Lower Canada the political differences were also racial differences, the French through their paper, *La Canadienne*, stirring up a distinctively national spirit. In both provinces alike the political discontent led to strong physical demonstrations, threats of annexation to the United States, the stoppage of supplies to Government, and strong representations to the authorities in Britain for the grant of responsible government. Matters came to a head when Papineau in the Lower province and Mackenzie in the Upper raised the standard of revolt, but not in concert. The risings were speedily put down, the constitutions were suspended, and Lord Durham came out as Governor-General with almost plenary powers in 1838.

The report that he drew up, describing the condition of the country and making recommendations for its improvement, is considered to be one of the ablest State documents ever submitted to Parliament. Constitution-makers go to it for inspiration. Its perusal is a tonic to those whose faith in the healing and ennobling power of popular imstitutions is weak. The chief lesson it conveys to us in India is that responsible government is a remedy and the only sure remedy for the evils arising from imperfect understanding between the government and the people. Existing defects in India are pointed to by opponents of progress as barring the way to a fuller measure of popular government. Whereas, if a second Lord Durham could now come out to report on Indian affairs, he would in all likelihood advocate the immediate grant of responsible government *as a cure* for the ills of the body politic.

Let us, as far as possible in his own words, give an idea of what Canada was like when he proposed his bold and startling reform. First as to education: "The continued negligence of the

"British Government left the mass of the people without any of the institutions, which would have elevated them in freedom and civilization. It has left them without the education and without the institutions of local self-government that would have assimilated their character and habits, in the easiest and best way, to those of the Empire." "It is impossible to exaggerate the want of education among the habitants. No means of instruction have ever been provided for them, and they are almost and universally destitute of the qualifications even of reading and writing." "A great proportion of the teachers could neither read nor write. . . . These ignorant teachers could convey no useful instruction to their pupils. These appointments were jobbed by the members among their political partisans; nor were the funds very honestly managed." Public administration was in a sad way: "But if such is the bad organisation and imperfection of the system at the seat of Government, it may be easily believed that the remainder of the province enjoyed no very vigorous or complete administration. In fact, beyond the walls of Quebec all regular administration of the country appeared to cease; and there literally was hardly a single public officer of the civil Government except in Montreal and Three Rivers, to whom any order could be directed." One other extract should suffice under this head. It refers to the district of Gaspè. "About the administration of justice therein I could hardly obtain any information; indeed on one occasion it being necessary, for some particular purpose, to ascertain the fact, inquiry was made at all the public offices in Quebec, whether or not there was any coroner for Gaspè. It was a long time before "any information could be got on this point, and it was "at last in some measure cleared up by the Accountant-"General discovering an estimate for the salary of "such an officer. The only positive information, "therefore, that I can give respecting the present ad-"ministration of justice in Gaspè is, that I received a "petition from the inhabitants praying that the Act "by which it is regulated might not be renewed." The system of justice was most unsatisfactory and juries had ceased to command confidence. Trade was backward, banking and other facilities were ill-organised, and internal communications were lacking in the remoter parts. As to municipal institutions, which are justly believed to be a good school of political education for the people, they were almost non-existent. "Lower Canada remains without munici-"pal institutions of local-self-government, which are "the foundations of Anglo-Saxon freedom and civiliza-"tion." "The inhabitants of Lower Canada were un-"happily initiated into self-government at exactly the "wrong end and those who were not trusted with the "management of a parish were enabled by their votes "to influence the destinies of a State." "In the rural "districts habits of self-government were almost un-"known, and education is so scantily diffused as to "render it difficult to procure a sufficient number of "persons competent to administer the functions that "would be created by a general scheme of popular "local control."

In fact, judged by every criterion applied in India, the French population of Quebec should have been pronounced to be utterly unfit even for representative institutions, let alone responsible government. Yet they are now amongst the most progressive and public-spirited people in the British Empire and have produced statesmen like Sir Wilfrid Laurier. Here are two extracts, from which it will appear how unpromising the material seemed at the time of Lord Durham. "But the French population of Lower Canada "possesses neither such institutions (municipal) nor "such a character (popular initiative). Accus-"tomed to rely entirely on the Government, it has "no power of doing anything for itself, much less of "aiding the central authority." "The institutions of "France during the period of the colonization of Cana-"da were, perhaps more than those of any other Eu-"ropean nation, calculated to repress the intelligence "and freedom of the great mass of the people. These "institutions followed the Canadian colonists across "the Atlantic. The same central, ill-organised, un-"improving and repressive despotism extended over "him. Not merely was he allowed no voice in the "government of his province or that of his rulers, but "he was not even permitted to associate with his neigh-"bours for the regulation of those municipal affairs "which the central authority neglected under the "pretence of managing." "The priest continued to "exercise over him his ancient influence. No general "provision was made for education, and as its "necessity was not appreciated, the Colonist made no "attempt to repair the negligence of his Government." "They made little advance beyond the first pro-"gress in comfort, which the bounty of the soil "absolutely forced upon them; under the same insti-"tutions they remained the same uninstructed, in-"active, unprogressive people."

More than all this was the natural enmity of the French and the English people, to which there is hardly a parallel in India. Sir James Craigh wrote: "The line of distinction between us is completely "drawn; friendship, cordiality are not to be found, "even common intercourse scarcely exists." From Lord Durham: "I found two nations warring in the "bosom of a single State. I found a struggle not of "principles but of races." "It is scarcely possible to "conceive descendants of any of the great European "nations more unlike each other in character and "temperament, more totally separated from each "other by language,laws, and modes of life or placed "in circumstances more calculated to produce "natural misunderstanding, jealousy or hatred." To show how intense political animosity was even after many years of responsible government, the following incident will suffice. In 1849 a Bill was passed giving compensation to people who had suffered losses for no fault of theirs during the preceding rebellion. Lord Elgin, then Governor-General, gave his assent to it. The Tory opposition, consisting mostly of English, raised the cry, 'no pay to rebels' and "some of them in their anger even "issued a manifesto in favour of annexation. The "Parliament House at Montreal was burnt down, a "great number of books and records destroyed, and "Lord Elgin grossly insulted for having assented to "the Bill."

What Canada obtained after strenuous struggles, the States of Australia got with comparative ease. In fact the colonial policy of Great Britain had been liberalised and responsible government was considered a proper solution of the problem of colonial administration. Most statesmen of the time believed, and were glad to believe that, once liberated from the shackles of the Colonial Office, the colonies would in course of time declare themselves independent of England. In this, however, events have proved them utterly mistaken. The grant of responsible government, wherever it has been made, has only strengthened the bond between the suzerain power and the subordinate but autonomous governments—a lesson which may well be borne in mind by those prophets of evil who prognosticate that in India political generosity will be met with ingratitude.

The Australian States attained responsible government between the years 1853 and 1859, Western Australia alone rising to the status in 1890. In 1850 the entire population in Australia was about 266,000; in 1860 it was 349,000. It is well-known that it started as a penal settlement. "For some years," says a historian, "the history of the infant settlement was that of a large gaol." It was in 1840 that the Secretary of State for the Colonies declared that no more convicts should be transported to Australia. The discovery of the first gold mine in 1851 ensured the economic prosperity of the colony. The population began to increase rapidly. It could not naturally have been marked by a high degree of culture or refinement, for it must have consisted to a large extent of adventurers, speculators and labourers. As was to be expected, politics in such a colony must be far different from politics elsewhere. The English party system and cabinet government took long to strike root. Between 1854 and 1890, the year when the Commonwealth was established, no Government could be sure of power for any length of time. "In South Australia there were forty changes of "Ministry in thirty-seven years. In New Zealand the "first four Ministries were strangled in their cradles, "and as late as August 1884 there came three weeks of "upheaval in Wellington in which three Ministries re-"signed in succession. Before the coming of Sir George "Turner in 1894 no Victorian Premier ever held the "reins for five years on end and only two Cabinets "had endured for as long as three. In New South "Wales Executives were even shorter-lived. Before "Reid was sworn in in 1894 only one Prime Minister, "Parkes, had managed to retain office in Sydney for "four years without break, Sir Henry once just con-"trived to do that; no one else stayed in for more "than two years and nine months." The instability of cabinets was only the reflection of the instability of political parties. It took long for these to be formed and organized and in the interval there were humours of political life of which it is very interesting to read. Mr. Reeves writes as follows: "At public meetings "candidates were pledged on certain prominent ques-"tions, and were usually accounted as owing allegi-"ance to this or that leader. But the opportunities of "disloyalty were innumerable, and full advantage "was taken of them. Men would keep platform "pledges to the letter and break them in spirit,—"could even, thanks to ignorance or apathy amongst "their constituents, ignore them altogether. There "was very little direct corruption; but unscrupulous "men would support Ministries for what grants "they hoped to get for their districts. Men still "more unscrupulous joined or deserted parties simply "in the hope of office. There were members avowedly "independent, who were occasionally the most honour-"able men in public life, but more often the reverse. "On the whole, the experience of parliamentary parties "without tight bonds and lasting lines of cleavage was "depressing to most of those behind the scenes. It was "emphatically a life in which it was wise to remember "that your enemy might some day be your friend, "while your friend would probably become your "enemy."

In South Africa too the success of responsible government has been remarkable. There were many who predicted disaster when the Government of Sir Henry Campbell-Bannerman had the courage to carry out their promise of autonomy to the newly-conquered Boer States. Their pastoral occupations, crude ideas, ignorance and general lack of refinement, taken along with their recent enmity to the British, no doubt were strong grounds for misdoubting the results of the great constitutional experiment. Still if we omit the outbreak of Hertzogism and of the serious education trouble it caused, the South African States, especially after the Union, have had a career of progress and prosperity. Their loyalty during the present war, notwithstanding the rebellion of De Wet, is a great tribute to the popularity of the free potitical institutions that Great Britain has allowed them to enjoy.

ENGLAND

Those that would deny to India the boon of self-government fix their gaze exclusively on the darker features in the condition of her people. If a similar one-sided examination were to be made of any country, it would be easy to draw a harrowing picture. Take England herself, where popular liberty has found such a congenial home for a long time now. Before 1832 her political condition was notoriously backward. Parliament scarcely represented the people. Jobbing and corruption were rife. The masses were uneducated (the Education Act was only passed in 1870) and could not cast votes with any intelligent understanding of what they were doing. If, as Mr. Curtis says in *The Problem of the Commonwealth*, "national self-government depends not upon "the handful of public men needed to supply cabinets "and parliaments, but on the electorate, on the fitness "of a sufficient proportion of the people themselves to "choose rulers able to rule," England's fitness for self-government is of very recent date indeed. A parliamentary Commission which reported in 1835 gives a most unflattering description of the condition of municipalities and boroughs at the time. Three extracts are sufficient as a sample. They are long, but considering how the shortcomings of local bodies in India are made the occasion for assailing the national character and pronouncing an adverse judgment on the aptitude of Indians for autonomy, it is necessary to give conclusive evidence that all mankind, including the portion which inhabits the home of freedom, is tarred with the same brush. Our authority is the standard work on *Local Government in England* by Redlich and Hirst.

"The corporations look upon themselves and are "considered by the inhabitants as separate and exclusive bodies; they have powers and privileges "within the towns and cities from which they are "named, but in most places all identity of interest "between the corporation and the inhabitants has "disappeared. Some corporations are occasionally spoken of as exercising their privileges through "a popular body, but in the widest sense in which the "term popular body is used in regard to corporate

" towns, it designates only the whole body of freemen; " and in most towns the freemen are a small number, " compared with the respectable inhabitants in- " terested in their municipal government and possess- " ing every qualification, except a legal one, to take " a part in it. In Plymouth, where the population, " including Devonport, is more than 75,000, the num- " ber of freemen is only 437, and 145 of these are non- " resident. In Norwich, the great majority of the in- " habitant householders and rate-payers are excluded " from the corporate body; while paupers, lodgers, " and others, paying neither rates nor taxes, are ad- " mitted to the exercise of the functions of freemen, " and form a considerable portion of the corporation. " In Ipswich, containing more than 20,000 inhabitants, " the resident freemen form about one fifty-fifth part " of the population. Of these more than one-third are " not rated, and of those who are rated many are ex- " cused the payment of their rates. About one-ninth " of the whole are paupers. More than eleven- " twelfths of the property assessed in this borough be- " longs to those who are excluded from the corpora- " tion. All the inhabitants whose rent exceeds £ 4 per " annum are taxed under a Local Act for municipal " purposes. Of these who are so taxed, less than one- " fifteenth are freemen. The assessed taxes paid in " the borough exceed £ 5,000 *per annum*. The amount " paid by all the corporate bodies is less than one- " twentieth of the whole."

"Few corporations admitted any positive obliga- " tion to expend surplus revenues upon public objects. " Such expenditure was regarded 'as a spontaneous " act of private generosity, rather than a well-con- " sidered application of the public revenue,' and the "credit which the close body would claim in such a "case was 'not that of judicious administrators but "of public benefactors.' The financial picture may "be completed by one more citation from the Report: "In general the corporate funds are but partially ap-"plied to municipal purposes, such as the preserva-"tion of the peace by an efficient police, or in watch-"ing or lighting the town, etc.; but they are frequently "expended in feasting, and in paying the salaries of "unimportant officers. In some cases, in which the "funds are expended on public purposes, such as "building public works, or other objects of local "improvement, an expense has been incurred much "beyond what would be necessary if due care had "been taken. This has happened at Exeter, in con-"sequence of the plan of avoiding public contract, "and of proceeding without adequate estimates. These "abuses often originate in the negligence of the cor-"porate bodies, but more frequently in the opportunity "afforded to them of obliging members of their own "body, or the friends and relations of such members."

"In conclusion, we report to Your Majesty that "there prevails amongst the inhabitants of a great "majority of the incorporated towns a general and, "in our opinion, a just dissatisfaction with their "municipal institutions, a distrust of the self-elected "municipal councils, whose powers are subject to no "popular control, and whose acts and proceedings, "being secret, are unchecked by the influence of "public opinion; a distrust of the Municipal Magis-"tracy, tainting with suspicion the local administra-"tion of justice, and often accompanied with contempt "of the persons by whom the law is administered; "a discontent under the burthens of local taxation, "while revenues that ought to be applied for the "public advantage are diverted from their legitimate "use and are sometimes wastefully bestowed for the "benefit of individuals, sometimes squandered for "purposes injurious to the character and morals of "the people. We therefore feel it to be our duty to "represent to Your Majesty that the existing munici-"pal corporations of England and Wales neither "possess nor deserve the confidence or respect of Your "Majesty's subjects, and that a thorough reform must "be effected before they can become, what we humb-"ly submit to Your Majesty they ought to be, useful "and efficient instruments of local government."

The following is the authors' comment: "When "one comes to examine the facts set out in this "Report, one cannot but wonder how such abuses "could have been tolerated for generations and cen-"turies in a land whose constitution was regarded by "some of its greatest statesmen and thinkers as an "embodiment of political justice and political wisdom. "For the picture presented by the Report is that of a "complete breakdown of administrative efficiency, "joined with a decay of the elementary rules of local "self-government. These symptoms, as the Commis-"sioners clearly show, were not natural, but were the "artificial product of a system of political corruption "erected and kept up by the ruling oligarchy. This "oligarchy had copied and improved upon the example "set by the Crown in the days of the Tudors and "Stuarts and had deliberately degraded the organiza-"tion of local government for political purposes."

A critic who saw only the evil side of things might likewise be surprised at the fact that the great measures for the emancipation of woman and the removal of the disabilities of the Catholics are not many decades old. He would express stern disapprobation of the political caucuses and party organizations which twist and misrepresent the important issues which the voter has to settle at a general election, but which he cannot understand in their real bearings, so much is he mystified and confounded by the interested representations that are made to him. Our pessimistic friend would be scandalised by the sale of titles and honours which seems to go on, whichever of the great parties is in power. The luxuries of the rich and the corruption of high life would form a formidable count in his indictment. The disclosures of the divorce court and the enormous extent to which betting is allowed under one form or another are aspects of social life which would shock and sadden him. When he came to consider the industrial organization he would be horrified by the immoralities of crowded factory-life and the frequent strikes and combinations that threaten the very foundation of the country's prosperity. When, depressed by all this and sick at heart, he came to a contemplation of the drink evil and the brutalisation attendant on it and the horrible condition of the slums with their dirt and poverty and ungodliness, he might well throw up his hands in despair and exclaim that the people of England should not be left to their own devices. So does an unrelieved enumeration of the weaknesses of private and public life in India produce the impression that her people have no redeeming virtues which by cultivation and constant exercise will enable them to sustain the burden of self-government.

FITNESS

GENERAL

In spite of the vicissitudes of fortune through which our country has passed, the great Dravidian, Aryan and Mahomedan civilizations are found in vigour, if not in their pristine purity. Each one of these civilizations has developed forms of government and systems of administration which have been productive of beneficent results to the people. Judged by modern standards they might be pronounced to lack the elements of strength and thoroughness. Nor do they appear to have given rise to democratic or popular forms of organization of the kind that we are familiar with to-day. Self-government then, in the sense of the power to develop an indigenous polity and find an indigenous agency to maintain it, has always been with us. It may have been overborne at times and not had free play, it may have degenerated under stress of adversity, it may have left the people weak, disorganised and helpless before external force; but it has always been there. The numerous Indian States carry on before our eyes the ancient traditions, transformed, it is true, in great measure and adapted to the special needs of the British pattern, but still kept alive by age-long aptitudes. In our own time the work done in these territories by some diwans and administrators within the limitations to which they are subject can bear comparison with the great deeds of Western statesmen in British India.

IN HIGH EXECUTIVE OFFICE

Whenever opportunity has been afforded, Indians have shown that they can work modern institutions in the modern spirit. In the executive, no less than in the judicial department, officers of the Provincial

Civil Service recruited by competition have proved themselves, man for man, the peers of their brethren in the Indian Civil Service. The Indians who were first appointed to the Council of the Secretary of State for India have elicited warm appreciation from no less a judge of men than Lord Morley. Lord Minto and Lord Hardinge have in turn borne generous testimony to the assistance they derived from the advice and co-operation of their Indian Ministers. The late Mr. Krishnaswamy Aiyar of Madras, the first Indian on that side of the country to whom a statue was erected by public subscription in which Europeans and Indians joined, has been the recipient of posthumous tributes from his European colleagues, which are remarkable as much for the admiration which they convey as for the note of personal attachment which they strike. To Mr. Gokhale, who struck the imagination of the English people in many ways, was reserved the unique honour of discussing affairs of high international moment, albeit in an informal way, with the Government of South Africa. This difficult and delicate task he performed with such ability, fairness and statesmanlike grasp of the issues involved that he earned the gratitude and admiration of all parties concerned.

Speaking on the proposal to appoint Indians to executive councils, Lord Morley said (1908): "We are not altogether without experience, because "a year ago, or somewhat more, it was my good for-"tune to be able to appoint two Indian gentlemen to "the Council of India sitting at the India office. "Many apprehensions reached me as to what might "happen. So far, at all events, those apprehensions "have been utterly dissipated. The concord between "the two Indian members of the Council and their "colleagues has been unbroken, their work has been "excellent, and you will readily believe me when I "say that the advantage to me of being able to ask "one of these two gentlemen to come and tell me "something about an Indian question from an Indian "point of view, is enormous. I find in it a chance of "getting the Indian angle of vision, and I feel some-"times as if I were actually in the streets of Calcutta." Arguing for the appointment of Indians to executive councils, Lord Morley said (1909): "You make an "Indian a Judge of the High Court, and Indians have "even been acting Chief Justices. As to capacity, who "can deny that they have distinguished themselves as "administrators of Native States, where far more "demand is made on their resources, intellectual and "moral?" Mr. Charles Roberts, at a banquet given in honour of Sir K. G. Gupta in 1905, said: "When Sir Krishna first took his seat at the "Council table, Lord Morley's innovation of appoint-"ing Indian gentlemen as members of the Council "was still an experiment. It was not an experiment "to-day. It was now an undoubted success, accepted "as a matter of course. That Indians should be on "the Council was not merely desirable. It was, he "believed, indispensable for the right government of "India." Speaking at the United Service Club at Simla in 1910, Lord Minto said: "Mr. Sinha is the "first Indian colleague of the Viceroy. It is quite "unnecessary for me to remind you of the great posi-"tion his distinguished and exceptional abilities "had obtained for him at the Calcutta bar, and, "gentlemen, I cannot let this opportunity pass with-"out bearing testimony to the able assistance he has "rendered to the Government of India and thanking "him for the absolute fairness and broad-minded "patriotism, which has always characterised the "advice I have so often sought from him."

The *Pioneer* wrote thus of Sir S. P. Sinha when he resigned his seat on the Viceroy's Council: "That "Mr. Sinha has performed his duties as part of "the Government of India conscientiously, faithfully "and with no small measure of success, that his "advice, loyally and straightforwardly given, has "been of the utmost value to his colleagues, will "readily be acknowledged by the whole official world "of Simla, who will be the first to regret his severance "from the inner Councils of the Government, while "recognising the personal sacrifices Mr. Sinha has "made in consenting to become the instrument where-"by an importent constitutional precedent has been "established." Sir Valentine Chirol wrote in the *Times*: "Mr. Sinha's resignation is much to be regretted in "the public interest; for his discharge of the duties "attaching to his post has gone far to reconcile those "who, like myself, had misgivings as to the wisdom "of calling any Indian into the Viceroy's Executive "Council, and chiefly on the very grounds which "have been erroneously suggested as an explanation "of Mr. Sinha's resignation."

Lord Hardinge paid the following tributes of praise to Sir Syed Ali Imam: "As for Sir Ali Imam, "I can only speak of him as a colleague imbued with "the highest sense of duty, patriotism and loyalty. "Not only by his actual service as head of the legis-"lative department, but also by his constant helpful-"ness, and loyal but straightforward advice, he has "been of the utmost advantage and assistance to me "and my Government. Now that he will be retiring "into private life, I wish him all success and happi- "ness." "To me personally he has constantly given the "most helpful advice, and I think our colleagues will "all bear witness to the great assistance he has ren- "dered to the Council over many difficult and knotty "problems. And remember that we have been through "no ordinary times. The stress of war has brought "anxieties in its turn to which our predecessors were "strangers and through them all it has been to us of "the utmost benefit to know from a distinguished "Indian at first hand how the varying aspects of our "different problems would strike the mind of various "sections of educated India. As a member of my "Council, I repeat, the presence of Sir Ali Imam has "been an asset of the utmost value and it was a "source of unmitigated satisfaction to me the other "day to pay him the greatest compliment at my dis- "posal by appointing him Vice-President of my "Council. His tenure of office has coincided, too, with "a great deal of difficult and important work in his "own particular department, and our war legislation "has attained to a volume of quite respectable dimen- "sions. Many questions of great technique and diffi- "culty have had to be solved and it is not only the "actual legislation that has been placed upon the "statute book, but a tremendous variety of problems "in which the other departments of the Government "have found themselves involved that have required "the help and guidance of the Legislative Department "under the auspices of Sir Ali Imam for their solu- "tion."

At the memorial meeting held at Madras in 1912 in honour of the late Mr. V. Krishnaswami

Iyer, Sir Murray Hammick said: "My first acquaintance with Mr. Krishnaswami Iyer was in his work in the Legislative Council, when his genius and sound judgment impressed us all. His mastery over the details of complicated matters astonished every one. Then later, when he became a member of the Executive Council, I had the honour of regarding him as a trusted friend, and for one year I had the pleasure of almost daily conversation and intercourse with him. I learnt to admire his genius, his extraordinary quickness, and above all his intense anxiety to be just to all men, and to do what he thought best for the welfare and advancement of his country. Generous in admiration of others, and full of sympathetic concern for his friends, his companionship will be to me one of the pleasantest of memories. I have thought his character was much like that which the stoic Emperor of Rome ascribed to his father, *viz.*, indifferent to compliment, pertinacious in his inquiries, loyal to his friends, and a wise counsellor."

Sir John Atkinson said at the same meeting: "My acquaintance with the late Mr. Krishnaswamy Iyer dates from a comparatively recent period, not more than five years back. But it is a matter of melancholy satisfaction to me that what was begun as a mere official acquaintance across the table of the Legislative Council chamber very rapidly developed into a friendship, the remembrance of which will always be among my cherished possessions. There are many others whose intimacy with Mr. Krishnaswamy Iyer was of far longer standing and of far closer a character than mine, but to me too it has been given to feel the fire of brain and glow of "heart that gave to Mr. Krishnaswamy Iyer so "strong and so winning a personality. It was of "course mainly in official paths that we were brought "together. He had no administrative experience "when he joined the Government. As he himself "said to me a day or two after that event he was only "a learner. But what a learner! It was astonishing "how rapidly he mastered not only the methods of "Secretariat procedure, but the substance and intri-"cacies of all the many complicated questions "submitted to him. It was in consonance with his "character that he should be rapid in making up "his mind, tenacious of his opinion and forceful "in supporting it. Yet he was always ready to hear, "most anxious always to look at every aspect of a "question, and incapable of taking a narrow or one-"sided view—a man 'that executed judgment and "that sought the truth'." It is not necessary for me "to speak at length regarding his work as member "of the Executive Council. It was its high quality "that makes our loss to-day so great. We have lost a "colleague who combined in himself all the qualities "that make for administrative success, who could ill "be spared and whose place it will, indeed, be hard to "fill. But great as were the qualities of his intellect, I "would rather pay my tribute to his character. It was "that which made him such a power for good not only "in Madras but throughout India. His ideals were so "lofty, his desire to rise to their level so passionate. "With him practice and precept ever went hand in "hand. He could not bear with the Laodicean tem-"perament. It was anathema to him. Mr. Krishna-"swami Iyer's restless energy, exercised, as it always "was, in the cause of what he believed to be right, "was one of the most admirable traits in his fine "character."

LEGISLATIVE COUNCILS

In the Legislative Councils the people's representatives have conducted themselves with moderation and self-restraint, and although they have chafed at the restrictions placed upon their activity and usefulness, their resentment has on no occasion broken out in any of those disorderly or violent forms which disfigure the annals of the legislatures of England and of the Dominions. Lord Hardinge has more than once borne high testimony to their work. Their criticism and advice have not been without effect on the policy and administration of the country. But so high is the expectation which the public entertain now-a-days of the legislative councils, and so keen is their sense of the impotence of their representatives from a constitutional point of view, that nothing can satisfy them hereafter short of the power of regulating the policy, disposing of the finances and controlling the executive. Said Lord Hardinge :

"I think I may say with some pride and satis- "faction that the debates that have taken place have "reached a far higher standard of statesmanship and "efficiency than has ever been previously attained. "They have taken place with a self-restraint and "a mutual courtesy and good fellowship that "might well be a model to all legislative bodies." "I think I can say from experience gained in "different parts of the world that this Council is "second to none in the dignity of its proceedings and "the good feeling that animates its members."

LOCAL SELF-GOVERNMENT

As regards municipalities and local boards, our record has been distinctly good. It was perhaps lucky that we began our career in local self-government with a large measure of control vested in the central government, for we have been saved from those depths of inefficiency and corruption into which the possession of unrestrained power seems to have thrown similar bodies in Great Britain. But the continuance of minute control and supervision long after the years of probation have passed, is a serious check on the growth of self-governing bodies, and it is now fully recognised by Government that they should be released from leading strings, entrusted with more powers and endowed with greater financial resources.

BUT THE MASSES ?

Thus far we have endeavoured to show that there is a sufficiency of talent and public spirit to fill all the positions of trust and responsibility in the country and to work all the associations and institutions which conduce to the common welfare. There are some who will readily grant the truth of this proposition, but will say that it is the ignorant and helpless condition of the masses that bars the way to progress. It is true that millions of our people are without the rudiments of education, that they are poor and that politically they are without any experience. But is there any country in the world having a large population where the masses though literate, are in a position to exercise their franchise with discrimination ? Are they able to follow discussions of public questions intelligently, weigh the pros and cons and come to a decision?

Do they make their choice between the competing candidates on their merits? Are they not swayed by prejudice, liable to influence and misled by wirepullers? Says Lord Bryce: "Though it is usually assumed in "platform speeches that the audience addressed are "citizens of this attractive type, everybody knows "that in all communities, not only in Chicago but even "in Liverpool, let us say, or in Lyons, or in Leipzig, a "large proportion of the voters are so indifferent or so "ignorant that it is necessary to rouse them, to drill "them, to bring them up to vote." It is not true that in any country which is now self-governing the people obtained the franchise only after they had secured the blessings of universal education. After all, this objection does not proceed with grace from the members or representatives or apologists of the Indian Government. They have done little as yet towards making elementary education universal, and it is a double wrong to use the prevailing illiteracy as a reason for denying the people the privilege of choosing their own representatives to make the laws of the land.

CASTES AND CREEDS

Then it is said that there are serious differences of a social and religious kind, numerous castes and creeds, each conscious of its difference from the rest and averse from any association with them. This is unfortunately the case, but the difficulties caused by this defect are grossly exaggerated. It is not true that for political purposes our castes and creeds refuse to commingle. Animosities and jealousies are rapidly yielding to the influence of education and to the sense of common needs, and it is the part of statesmanship to provide occasion for the communities coming together for common purposes. Instead, the legislative councils have been made the cause of a separatist tendency between Hindus and Mahomedans, and in one province the separation has recently been extended to local bodies as well. It is to be hoped that this disintegrating principle will not be allowed into other provinces or in the case of other communities. Anyhow signs are not wanting that the leaders of opinion in these communities are coming to realize that the separation should be only for a time, after which in political and municipal matters all communal differences should be ignored. In Madras and parts of the Bombay Deccan the Brahman class has created a feeling of jealousy and distrust against itself. The non-Brahman, though in an overwhelming majority, finds his class without adequate representation in the services or in the professions, and believes that this result is due to the caste instinct of the Brahman who, having selfishly monopolised the advantages of education and social precedence in the past, is now equally selfishly enjoying its fruits by keeping members of other castes from approaching all modern avenues to preferment and distinction. It does not matter whether the Brahman secures the domination of his caste by deliberate and malicious conspiracy or by an instinctive spirit of exclusiveness which is his biological inheritance; the sense of injustice and long-continued wrong rankles equally, and to-day we have the heart-rending spectacle of certain leaders of the non-Brahman community opposing the political progress of the country on the ground that they must continue for a long time yet to depend on the impartiality and protection of the European officials from the arrogant ascendency of the Brahman. The ill-feeling came out in an ugly form when the Public Services Commission visited Madras and has since passed into an acute phase. Let us hope it is at its worst now. Two facts, however, seem to line the cloud with silver. The ascendency of the Brahman has given way in many places and is certain to be effaced in a generation. Large numbers both of the Brahman and the non-Brahman communities have seen the unwisdom of wrangling with one another to the merriment and advantage of third parties, and the good influence of these peacemakers and patriots is softening acerbity all round. One duty rests on the Brahman, as being the party having the advantage at present. He must recognise that the attitude of the non-Brahman is not only the natural but inevitable consequence of the past, and must be ready and willing in social relations to pay tender heed to the feelings of the non-Brahman, remembering always how keenly he himself feels the affronts, sometimes real but often fancied, of those whom he blames as unable to forget their political superiority. A little thing, said the poet, may harm a wounded man, and this saying has a physical and also a moral application. When the Mahomedans are grasping the hands of the Hindus in friendship, the non-Brahmans will not, we trust, stand apart from their brethren and cry out against the progress of the country.

A GLANCE ABROAD

After all this evil is not altogether absent from more fortunate countries. In England to-day no reform in education can be proposed without raising in an acute form what is known as the religious difficulty. Lord Haldane said only the other day that a great load of educational sin rested on the shoulders of many right reverend prelates and of nonconformists on this account. And complaints are not unknown that the aristocracy have almost a monopoly of facilities of attaining the great positions of public life, and that the sons of the poor, though endowed with brains, do not enjoy the share of the posts in public service to which they are entitled. For centuries Europe was deluged with blood by religious wars, and the persecution of the Jews by Christian communities, which only ceased the other day, is one of the foul stains on western civilization. England's record in this respect is not altogether white. Roman Catholics first, then Protestants, passed laws against their religious foes and persecuted them with a rancour scarcely less than any that the history of India can show. The fact is that religious toleration and complete religious freedom are principles of which human society had occasional glimpses in the ancient world, but which even Anglo-Saxon peoples have realised in their fulness only within the lifetime of the present generation. The history of India has periods, like those of Asoka and Akbar, in which those principles regulated not only the action of Governments but the social life of the people. No foreign authority is needed to impose them on the polity of India, just as it was not required for their evolution in England. Too many Indians believe without reason that in this matter they are in a special degree the accursed of creation, because they have been taught to believe so. Lest these should despise themselves as irredeemable, we shall present them with one extract out of many that are available to show how free and Protestant England could behave in a time not long past towards Catholic Ireland. Lord Dunraven writes in *Legacy of Past Years*: "The Penal Code came into existence under William "immediately after the Revolution, and was extended "under Anne and the first two Georges. It affected "all human action and endeavour in every form of "life. Catholics were prohibited from sitting in "Parliament, and were deprived of the franchise. "They were excluded from the Army, Navy, the "Magistracy, the Bar, the Bench. They could not "sit on Grand Juries or Vestries, or act as sheriffs or "solicitors. The possession of arms was forbidden "to them. They could not be freemen of any cor-"porate body, and were allowed to carry on trade only "on payment of various impositions. They could not "buy land nor receive it as a gift from Protestants; "nor hold life annuities or mortgages or leases for "more than thirty-one years, or any lease if the "profit exceeded one-third of the rent. Catholics "were deprived of the liberty to leave property in "land by will. Their estates were divided among all "their sons unless the eldest became a Protestant, "in which case the whole estate devolved upon him. "Any Protestant who informed upon a Catholic for "purchasing land became the proprietor of the estate. "No Catholic was allowed to possess a horse of "greater value than £5, and any Protestant could "take the horse for that sum. A Protestant woman "landowner was, if she married a Catholic, deprived "of her property; mixed marriages celebrated by a "Catholic priest were declared null. A wife or a "child professing Protestantism was at once taken "from under the Catholic husband or father's "control, and the Chancellor made an assignment of "income to them. Catholic children under age at "the time of the Catholic father's death were placed "under the guardianship of Protestants. Catholics "were excluded from seats of learning. They could not "keep schools or teach or act as guardians of child- "ren." If India has more of communal jealousy to-day than other countries, it only means that it requires greater circumspection in making the arrangements and greater safeguards. It cannot render the introduction of popular institutions impossible.

RACE

Defeated on all these counts, the opponent of Indian progress may seek shelter under the argument of race, believing that, as it is an unchangeable factor, the disqualification imposed by it is irremovable. Mr. Curtis, for example, contends that the Asiatic races do not yet possess the faculty of self-government, excepting perhaps the Japanese—the "perhaps" is meant to prove the extreme caution of his thought and reluctance to make any exception. God made the Westerns to rule and the Easterns to obey. They are the Kshatriyas and Shudras respectively of creation. What is it but a revival of the caste system without its spiritual sanction? "Race" is one of those ideas, difficult to analyse and difficult to define, which have come down to us from the past, breeding contempt and hatred between peoples, and used as if it were a charter from heaven by those who have succeeded to warn off those who wish to succeed. Even negroes and pariahs, when carefully educated, are capable of assimilating the civilization of Europe and following any profession with credit. Stress of circumstances may compel a pleasure-loving people to take to arms in self-defence or seek their fortune in wild and hazardous occupations. A hardy and warlike people may become through a long period of peace tillers of the soil or votaries of learning. Scientists and historians may have erudite theories on race and racial characteristics, but the soul of man will revolt against the unblest doctrine that one portion of mankind is for ever to rule and another portion of mankind is for ever to bend its neck to the yoke. Here are a few passages from thoughtful writers protesting against the eternity of this summary two-fold classification. Dr. Emil Reich, in his book called *Success among Nations*, says: "Amongst many latter-day historians it has been the "fashion to seek an explanation of national pre-emi-"nence in race. This method certainly has the ad-"vantage of flattering national vanity, but it cannot "claim any great scientific value, as the problems it "deals with, though expressed in a different set of "terms, are not brought any nearer solution. In nearly "every instance the racial threads from which a white "nation is woven are so inextricably intertwined that "it would be quite impossible to determine, even with "approximate exactitude, what is the predominant "element. Let us, then, at once set aside the hypo-"thesis of any peculiar virtue inherent in a particular "shade of complexion or variety of blood, and seek for "a far readier explanation of our facts in the physical "conditions under which these nations lived and had "their being. We shall then see why it is that the "conquering race is so often compelled to bow to the "civilization of the vanquished and advance along "their line of development. How often has this been "the case in Egypt, Babylonia, and even China!" Again: "The most ingenious books have been written

" endeavouring to apply the theory of race to the ex-
" planation of the rise of intellect among nations.
" But the racial theory has been ridden to death.
" After a long struggle, it is now being eventually
" abandoned by its most fanatical adherents in the
" ranks of modern historians. But the average man
" still pins his faith to it. The ordinary Englishman
" still attributes, and will continue to attribute, the
" success of his nation to the predominance
" of the Anglo-Saxon stock; there is something
" extremely flattering to national pride in the notion.
" It also permits of a rapid and complete annihilation
" of the so-called Latin races. The Frenchman is al-
" so fired by a kindred admiration of all that has
" issued from the Gallo-Roman blood. a theory which
" also allows of the equally rapid and complete dis-
" posal of all that is Teutonic and Anglo-Saxon. We
" have already shown how absolutely impossible and
" inapplicable such theories are in the scientific stu-
" dy of history. Race is quite impossible of identifica-
" tion, and where we can to some extent follow out
" the lines of ethnographical demarcation, it does not
" in any degree correspond with the national frontier.
" We must seek for some more substantial basis on
" which to found our theories of the causes of intel-
" lectual growth." Jean Finot has demonstrated in *Race Prejudice* the impossibility " of attributing
" immutable psychological qualities to certain peoples
" or races." "Their virtues and their vices," he concludes, " are only the effects of historic circumstances
" or of the influence of the *milieu*." "Savage peoples," he says, " enter triumphantly into our civilization
" just as civilised peoples fall back into barbarisms.
" . . ., Within the space of fifty years the Negroe

"have realised as much progress as many white "peoples have done in five or six centuries." "The "history of civilization is only a continual come and "go of peoples and races. All, without distinction "of their biological characteristics, are summoned to "this great struggle for life wherein we fight for "human progress and happiness. All the ethnical "elements can take part in it, all can contend for "places of honour in it. Such is the general import "of our biological and psychological equality, which "remains intact underneath all our superficial divi- "sions." "In one word, the term race is only a "product of our mental activities, the work of our "intellect, and outside all reality. . . . Races, as "irreducible categories, only exist as fictions in our "brains. They exist in us but not outside us."

Mr. John M. Robertson, M. P., in his paper on *The Rationale of Autonomy* contributed to the first Universal Races Congress held in 1911 writes : "It really "amounts to confessing that all peoples who have "not hitherto governed themselves are relatively "undeveloped ; that, in short, self-government is the "pre-requisite of any high level of social organization "and general capacity. This implication, however, "is not always avowed, even by the more thoughtful "exponent of imperialism in our own day ; and until "recent times it was rather the exception than the "rule of historians even to note that when, in ancient "Greece and Rome, an end was put to the life of free "discussion and political conflict, the general level "of human faculty began to sink. The truth that "the habit of constant debate and the perpetual prac- "tice of affairs are the vital conditions of intellectual "and moral betterment for communities as wholes, is

" still far short of being a current axiom. Yet it is proved " alike by the decay of the classic civilizations after " the ending of autonomy and by the advance of " modern civilization hand in hand with autonomy." " The contemporary problem may be put in a nut- " shell. Are the subject races of to-day progressing " or not? If yes, they must be on the way, however " slowly, to a measure of self-government. If not, " the domination of the advanced races is a plain " failure; and the talk of *beneficent rule* becomes an " idle hypocrisy." "But the first thing to be posited is " a warning that 'difficulty' and 'ill-preparedness' are " in no way special to the cases of tropical countries " and so-called 'backward' races. The critical pro- " cess applied to these cases by those who commonly " fall back on the formula of 'fitness' is extraordi- " narily imperfect. On their own view, those races " are 'fit' which have slowly attained self-govern- " ment after starting on the journey at a notably " low stage of 'fitness,' and undergoing on the way " all manner of miscarriages, including civil war. " Only by development out of unfitness, obviously, " is fitness attainable. Yet the bare fact of un- " fitness is constantly posited as if it were the fixed " antipodes of fitness. It is commonly put, for instance, " as the decisive and final anwer to any plea for the " gradual development of self-governing institutions " in India, that if India were evacuated by the British " forces there would ensue civil war, if not a new war " of conquest. That is of course an even superfluously " valid argument against the evacuation of India, " which no politician is known ever to have suggest- " ed. But it is put as if the bare potentiality were a " demonstration of the unfitness of the Indian peoples "collectively for any kind of institution tending ever "so remotely towards autonomy. Now, within the "English-speaking world, the mother country had "civil wars in the seventeenth and eighteenth cen-"turies; there was civil war between mother country "and colonies towards the end of the eighteenth; and "again within the independent United States and "within Canada in the nineteenth—all this in a "'race' that makes specially high claims to self-"governing faculty. On the imperialist principle, a "Planetary Angel with plenary powers would have "intervened to stop the 'premature experiment' of "Anglo-Saxon self-government at any one of the "stages specified—if indeed he had ever allowed it to "begin." "The demand that the latter shall maintain "an attitude of humble acquiescence for an indefinite "time in the hope that when they have ceased to ask "for anything they will spontaneously be given it, "is quite the most senseless formula ever framed in "any political discussion. Peoples so acquiescent "would be the most thoroughly unfit for self-govern-"ment that have yet appeared. They would be one "longer 'viable'."

Sir Charles Bruce, in his paper on "The Modern Conscience in relation to the Treatment of Dependent Peoples and Communities," contributed to the same Congress, says: "In conclusion it is submitted that "in the treatment of dependent peoples and communi-"ties the modern conscience rejects as a fallacy the "claim of western civilization to a monopoly of the "capacity of self-government based on an indivisible "inter-relation between European descent, Christian-"ity, and the so-called white colour. It recognises "that, while this inter-relation has evolved a capacity "for self-government in an appropriate environment, "a similar capacity has been evolved by an inter-"relation of other races, creeds and colours appro-"priate to other environments. It maintains, there-"fore, that the conflict between West and East must "be adjusted on the same principle that has adjusted "the conflicts of race and creed in the West, the "principle of freedom interpreted as liberty of person "and conscience and equality of opportunity for all, "without distinction of race, creed, or colour, under a "settled government." "History, reason, and recent "experience in Japan warn us that the adjustment "must be made not in the spirit of the popular refrain, "East is East and West is West, but in the spirit of "a nobler poetic formula :

"'God's in the Occident,
God's in the Orient.'

"This is the spirit of the modern conscience in "the treatment of dependent peoples and communities."

NOT YET

The theory of unfitness appears in another shape, not so uncompromising, but not less dangerous. The unfitness, say some critics, is not incurable ; in course of time, under careful and benevolent political education such as our slowly-broadening institutions afford, it is possible, though prophecy in such matters is proverbially foolish, that the people of India may become fit for self-rule. But that day is not yet. Wait, wait in patience. Then our mentors resort to metaphor. The way is long and weary, full of peril and adventure. Do you know how they toiled and travailed who went before you, what trials and tribulations they had to bear? Metaphor and proverb, fable and parable, history and epic, teach us a good deal; they give us warning and guidance. But they are not actual life, they cannot replace direct experience either for individuals or communities. The best training is obtained when you grapple with your difficulties by yourself, the highest and most useful part of education is self-education. The people of India will become fit for self-rule only by practising self-rule. There is no other way for it. They must conceive their aims and ideals, they must lay their plans and execute them, make mistakes and rectify them, incur losses and recoup them, encounter perils and overcome them. Mr. L. Curtis, in his book *The Problem of the Commonwealth*, writes: "In the "first place, the exercise of responsibility tends to in-"crease fitness for exercising it. As every one finds "in his own experience, it is in having to do things "that a man learns how to do them and develops a "sense of duty in regard to them. And that is why "political power is and ought to be extended to whole "classes of citizens, even when their knowledge "and sense of responsibility is still imperfectly "developed." True, this process should not begin too early; there must be a period of preliminary training. What is the period required? The answer is, till the necessary general intellectual and moral equipment is acquired, till the necessary political experience has been gained. Our contention is that we have this necessary equipment and experience. In so far as such comparison is possible, we cannot see that India is less fitted to-day than the Philippines for self-rule, nor that her general condition is much behind the condition of Canada or the other Dominions when they had the gift of responsible government, and we go further and say that England and

Japan appear to have had nearly as many shortcomings as India now has when they adopted a fully popular constitution. The Emperor of Japan took the great Charter oath in 1869; in 1881 he promised to grant a constitution in ten years; and in 1890 the first Imperial Diet was summoned. The Filipinos have had less than twenty years' schooling in civilized administration. Are Indians so much worse than the Filipinos, or is the school of British political institutions so much slower than that of American political institutions that it takes a century, and how much longer one cannot say, to complete the process of education in the one case which in the other is completed in twenty years? The first legislative council met in Canada in 1792. In fifty years full responsible government was granted. In New South Wales the first Parliament met in 1843. The first responsible ministry took office in 1856. Indians were first admitted to the legislative council in 1861, though it had been in existence for many years. It is not generally known, but it is a remarkable fact that, during this first period, when Europeans enjoyed the exclusive right of legislation for India, they conducted business in regular parliamentary style, with their own standing orders, calling the acts of the executive in question and carrying on debates which in their range and breezy freedom contrast markedly with the prudish and correct respectability of present-day proceedings. Beginning in 1861 on a scale which was caution itself, the non-official Indians admitted to the council being few and nominated, and the council itself never meeting except when there was a legislative measure to be placed before it, we did not take a second step till more than thirty years had passed. In 1892 after a good deal of popular agitation, the number of non-officials was increased slightly, they were still nominated in form, but practically elected by delegates of local bodies, a limited power of interpellation was given them, and the annual budget was placed before them for discussion, but it was not to be voted upon. Seventeen years passed and strong agitation had to be made before the third step was taken in 1909. This time local legislatures were to have non-official majorities, members in the councils could put supplementary questions and move resolutions on subjects of public interest, subject however to too many exceptions and to the further proviso that, even if accepted by the council, they were not to be binding on the executive. These reforms were introduced with a great fanfare of liberal sentiment, and generally hailed by the people as a substantial improvement. But the seven years that have passed since have been marked by an enormous advance of political thought and political ambition in the people, and the councils are spoken of by the advanced school as glorified debating clubs. In fact, the executive government is still practically master of the situation and carries measures in the teeth of public opposition. After fifty-five years people's representatives have still nothing like constitutional power in the land. Surely our progress is none too hurried. The foundations have had ample time to settle down and can now carry the full weight of the structure of self-government.

THE SCHEME

OUTLINE

We now come to a consideration of the actual demands that the leaders of the people make in the way of constitutional changes in the government. Till the Indian National Congress and the All-India Muslim League have met at Lucknow and adopted resolutions on the subject, no proposals can be said to carry the authority of the country's approval. But the executives of these great political organizations have formulated certain schemes, and at a joint meeting held recently in Calcutta have agreed to recommend a common scheme to their parent bodies at the coming session. This common scheme is still confidential, though the more important features have transpired. There is, besides, the memorandum of nineteen elected Indian members of the Viceroy's Legislative Council, which has been published. It is possible therefore to state with some degree of approximation the main demands that will be made in the name of the people by their representatives assembled in the Congress and in the League. For our purposes here the following outline may suffice as an anticipation.

The King-Emperor will govern India through a Viceroy assisted by an Executive Council composed of six persons, three Indian and three European. The European members will be appointed by the Viceroy, but need not be chosen from the Indian Civil Service or any other Service in India. The Indian members are to be elected by the elected members of the Viceroy's Legislative Council. The Council of the Secretary of State being abolished, and he being reduced to the status of the Colonial Secretary, all control over the Executive will be exercised by the Legislative Council in India. It will be enlarged to about 150, four-fifths of whom will be elected by the people of the country on a direct franchise, Mahomedans being entitled to a certain percentage of these seats through separate electorates of their own. The members of the Executive Council will be *ex officio* members of the Legislative Council and the Viceroy will nominate the remaining members from officials as well as non-officials. The Council will enjoy the power of legislation for all India subject to the veto of the Viceroy and to disallowance by the Crown within a certain period. The Council will be competent to interpellate the Executive in the same way as members of Parliament do in England, and to pass resolutions which may be vetoed by the Viceroy in Council but shall be binding on the Executive Government if reaffirmed substantially after one year of such veto. The Council will elect its own Speaker. Its duration like that of the members of the Executive Government will be five years. The Viceroy may dissolve it before its time, but he must summon another Council within a certain period. No more than one year should elapse betwen one meeting of the Council and another. As to finance, the Executive Government will frame the proposals for each year which will be discussed by the Legislative Council and must be passed in the shape of money Bills. The expenditure on the army and the navy, however, shall not be subject to the sanction of the legislature. The Government of the Provinces is to be more or less on the same lines. Each Province should have a Governor appointed directly by the Crown. Provincial legislation will be subject to the veto of the Governor and to disallowance by the Governor-General. The financial relations between the Government of India and the Provincial Governments are not fully worked out; but the general idea is that there should be a division of the revenues into Imperial and Provincial, and that for deficiencies in the Imperial budget, the Provinces shall be called upon to make contributions on principles to be settled from time to time.

SHORT OF RESPONSIBLE GOVERNMENT

It will be seen from this outline that the scheme falls short of responsible government as understood in the Dominions. In the first place, the financial antonomy is subject to a serious deduction. But the more important difference is in the relation of the executive to the legislature. The executive need not necessarily command the confidence of a majority of the legislature; and it will not go out of office by reason of an adverse vote. It has apparently no collective responsibility and, as there is no one corresponding to the Premier in the British system, it is obvious that the head of the Government will be the real, and not merely the nominal, head of the executive. Though the subordination of the executive to the legislature is not secured so fully as under what is known as responsible government, still it is secured in considerable measure by the provision as to the binding nature of twice-passed resolutions and the election of half their number by the elected members of the legislature. Also there is the five year limit to the duration of their office. That these safeguards are not altogether shadowy will be clear from the italicised portion of the following opinion of Dr. A. B. Keith on the executive governments of the South African Provinces. "The members of the Committee need not even "be members of the Provincial Council; and they hold "their offices from general election to general elec- "tion independently of the views of the Council. So "that there is no responsible government in the "management of the affairs of the province, *though "there is of course some approach to it in that the members "are elective and not permanent.*" It is thus clear that the framers of the scheme have deliberately avoided the full parliamentary system as unsuitable to the present condition of India. Opinions may differ as to the wisdom of this judgment; but there is one weighty consideration in its favour. The parliamentary system is only possible on two conditions—that there should be two parties in the chamber and that there should be only two parties. Bryce says: "Government of the English cabinet type is essenti- "ally party government. That is to say, it has been "so hitherto both in England and wherever else it had "been tried. And no one has yet shown how it can be "made to work otherwise." To the same effect, Dicey: "Now, that the existence of two leading parties and "of two such parties only in England has favoured the "development of English constitutionalism is past "denial." Also Lowell: 'If the existence of a res- "ponsible ministry normally involves government by "party, it also requires as a condition of success that "there shall be only two parties." Though many States have imitated the English cabinet system, it has not produced equally happy results, because there are more than two parties in them and they are grouped round persons competing with one another for place and power rather than based on a difference of principles or programmes. Even in England after the advent of the Irish Nationalists and more recently the Labour members, the party system has ceased to be as advantageous as it was before. The exigencies of the present war have obliterated the distinctions of party, and party spirit is now stigmatised as the opposite of patriotism. It is at least open to doubt whether the party system will recover its former strength and vigour in England. Considerations like these may give pause to those that would construct a form of government dependent for its full success on a true party system. No one can predict whether we shall ever evolve two great schools of political thought paying homage to two fundamentally opposed principles. The probability is, we shall have many parties without any dividing lines capable of clear definition. Cabinets formed in such conditions cannot govern long or with vigour. In all likelihood we shall have a reproduction of the 'spoils' system, and an utter enfeeblement and corruption of the public services, with its inevitably disastrous reaction on the character of the people at large. Moreover, there is a special danger in India of which an indication is given in the subjoined passage from Lowell's *Government of England*: "For the same reason there is grave danger when "the lines of cleavage of the parties coincide with those "between the different social classes in the community, "because one side is likely to believe that the other is "shaking the foundations of society, and passions are "kindled like those that blaze in Civil War. This is "true whenever the parties are separated by any of the "deeper feelings that divide mankind sharply into "groups; and especially when two or three such feel-

"ings fall on the same channel. The chief difficulty "with Irish Nationalism, as a factor in English poli-"tics, lies in the fact that to a great extent the line of "cleavage is at once racial, religious, social and econo-"mic. In order that the warfare of parties may "be not only safe but healthy, it must be based "upon a real difference of opinion about the needs "of the community as a whole. In so far as it is "waged, not for public objects, but for the private "gain, whether of individuals, or of classes, or of "collective interests, rich or poor, to that extent poli-"tics will degenerate into a scramble of self-seekers." There is no doubt the party system kept within limits is useful; but it has an inherent tendency to get out of control. In America it has assumed portentous dimensions and has organizations almost rivalling the State itself. In England its evil influence is so far felt that Prof. Dicey strikes a note of alarm. "The greatest political danger," he says, "with which "England is now threatened is the inordinate influence "of party mechanism." In another place, he says: "The party machine is regarded with suspicion "and often with detestation by public-spirited citizens "of the United States. Coalitions, log-rolling, and par-"liamentary intrigues are in England diminishing "the moral and political faith in the House of Com-"mons. Some means must, many Englishmen be-"lieve, be found for the diminution of evils which are "under a large electorate the natural, if not the "necessary, outcome of our party system."

SELF-GOVERNMENT OR HOME RULE?

At this point reference may be conveniently made to a dispute which has drawn more attention than it deserves. Does the scheme amount to Self-government? May it be fitly called Home Rule? When the leaders of the Indian National Congress declared the goal of their political aspirations to be "a system of government similar to that enjoyed by the self-governing members of the British Empire," or, for short, Colonial Self-government, they did so because the Dominions had had a certain form of government for some time and it was capable of more or less exact description. Home Rule for Ireland had not been accomplished, if indeed it can be said to be accomplished now. Strictly speaking, self-government shoul mean absolute independence; in fact, one of the chapters of Mr. Curtis's book is headed "How the Dominions stopped short of self-government." For ordinary purposes, either expression will do in the sense of a substantial measure of autonomy in internal matters. Which of them shall we take? It is a matter of individual preference. 'Self-governing' India is surely better than 'Home Ruling' India. A 'Self-governmenter' would be an impossible person, whereas a 'Home Ruler' comes to you at least with a pleasing name. When Lord Durham used the phrase 'responsible government,' he did not mean what it has since come to mean in the case of the Dominions. He excluded not only military matters and the external relations of the colonies, but even trade regulations and the disposal of public lands. In point of fact, Imperial control has been exercised in recent yeas in respect of the following: (1) some matters affecting the internal affairs of the Dominion; (2) native affairs; (3) the immigration of coloured races; (4) treaty relations and foreign affairs; (5) trade and currency; (6) merchant shipping; (7) copy-right; (8) divorce and status; (9) military and naval defence. Under the Government of Ireland Act recently passed, but now under suspension, the Irish can send 42 members to the Parliament of the United Kingdom; the Executive Government will be carried on in the name of the King by the Lord Lieutenant of Ireland who is to appoint his ministers from the majority in the Irish Parliament. The power of the Irish Parliament is subject to a large list of exceptions, finance being regulated by complicated adjustments between the two Governmets. The exceptions are, briefly, all external relations, the Army and the Navy, Dignities or Titles of honour, Treason, Naturalization, Trade, Light-houses, Coinage and Currency, Weights and Measures, copyright and Patents. Other reservations for a certain period are Land Purchase, National Insurance, Old Age Pensions, Labour Exchanges (in these matters the British Acts apply); Collection of Taxes; Constabulary; Post Office Savings Banks; Trustee Savings Banks; Friendly Societies; Public Loans (before the Act). It will thus be seen that on the whole the scheme of the Congress for India would rank distinctly below the colonial standard and allowing for the peculiar intricacy of the relations between England and Ireland, even below the Irish standard. Judged by this test, neither the expression Self-government nor the expression Home Rule will apply to our case in their specific meaning. In a loose way both may be used. As for the unhappy associations of Home Rule, there is hardly any force in the objection. The Britisher is a hardened political by now, and no mere wôrd will scare him, especially when he is threatened with Home Rule for England, Home Rule for Scotland and Home Rule for Wales as well. On the contrary, the use of the word Self-government in the Congress Constitution constitues a great recommendation.

POSSIBILITY OF GROWTH

The general rule of constitutional growth in the British Empire is, to mention only three distinctive stages, from Crown Colony administration through representative institutions to responsible government. Lord Durham in his famous report greatly discounted the second stage which only gave occasion for bitter conflicts between the legislature and the executive. The passage in which he expressed this opinion is famous and has been made still more famous by being used by Mr. Winston Churchill in introducing a measure in the House of Commons for giving responsible government to the Transvaal and the Orange River Colony. "It is difficult to understand how any English statesman could have imagined that representative and irresponsible government could be successfully combined. There "seems, indeed, to be an idea that the character of "representative institutions ought to be thus modified "in colonies; that it is an incident of colonial "dependence that the officers of government should "be nominated by the Crown without any reference "to the wishes of the community whose interests are "entrusted to their keeping. It has never been very "clearly explained what are the Imperial interests "which require this complete nullification of representative government. But if there is such a necessity it is quite clear that a representative government in a colony must be a mockery and a source "of confusion, for those who support this system have "never yet been able to devise or exhibit in the "practical working of colonial government any "means for making so complete an abrogation of "political influence palatable to the representative "body." This opinion, however, was challenged in the debate that followed by Sir Charles Dilke, who characterized it as a very rash assertion and propounded the illiberal doctrine that representative institutions formed the only possible government where there was an overwhelming black or native majority. Without being deterred, however, by this doctrine, it is permissible to inquire whether the responsibility of a government to the legislature can be secured only by a system of ins and outs, technically known as responsible government. The system of mutual checks between the different elements that compose the sovereign power depends on the relative strength and prestige of those elements. To adopt the English system wholesale would be to assume that those elements have in India the same relative position that they have in England. This assumption is not justified. The single fact that the representative of the Crown is to preside over the executive government and to have a very large power of veto over legislation is enough to upset all calculations made on that assumption. There is also the great example of the United States, in which a highly popular form of government exists, although the executive cannot be removed by a vote of the legislature. If the provisions as to interpellation, resolutions, financial control and the election of half the executive prove in actual experience insufficient to secure the subordination of the executive, the expedient might be tried of passing a vote of censure which should involve the dismissal of the minister or ministers concerned. A distinction might also be developed, if necessary, between legislative measures relating purely to the internal affairs of the country and legislative measures in which imperial interests and the prerogatives of the Crown were involved; the Viceroy's power to veto in the case of the former class being restricted in the same way as in the case of resolutions, while it remained absolute in the case of the latter class.

OBJECTIONS

NATIVE STATES EXCLUDED

Let us now deal with some objections that are made to this scheme of reform in the constitution of India. The exclusion of Native States from part or lot in it strikes the attention first. Quite recently the Chiefs and Princes of India have declared through the mouth of one of their ablest and most enlightened representatives that, as they do not wish in any way to interfere in the affairs of British India, so they do not wish British India to interfere in their affairs. Even without such a statement the leaders of the Congress movement have from the beginning steadily kept the politics of Native States out of their programme. If a large measure of self-government be granted after the war, British India will progress so rapidly that the Native States will be pressed forward by their subjects along the same path. The wiser princes may earn a great name by giving their people free constitutions and their example must drag the others behind sooner or later. Further developments belong to a distant future and need not trouble us here.

NO SECOND CHAMBER

Strong exception may be taken to the absence of a second Chamber from the scheme. Its authors would appear indeed to reject the experience of all countries which have followed English institutions. Excepting the majority of the provinces in the Dominion of Canada and the provinces under the Union of South Africa, the British Colonies and States have set up a bi-cameral system. The exceptions above named may partially justify the scheme so far as the Local. Governments are concerned, but the Government of India which resembles the Federations will stand quite alone in the whole world with a single Chamber. The failure of the House of Lords in England has apparently influenced the minds of public men in India, but the proposal to abolish the Lords has not received much support except among the Radicals and Labourites. The general opinion would appear to favour the reform of the Upper House rather than its extinction. Outside Great Britain, second Chambers have not been so unpopular. At the worst some have been ineffective. In some Australian States, they take a considerable share of legislative work. In consequence there is frequent disagreement between the Houses and elaborate provisions have been enacted to get over deadlocks. As Bryce says, popular governments do not follow the same paths in all the countries or develop good and evil in the same degree. Experience alone can show how a uni-cameral system will work in India. It is probable that the elected majority will take many years to assert itself. In the meantime the executive government and the nominated members may serve to some extent the purpose of the second Chamber, delaying and amending or at least compelling the consideration of those aspects of measures which may escape the attention of the homogeneous majority. Anyhow those that would have a fully elected Parliament would now find greater difficulty in carrying their point than if there were a second House. Those that interest themselves in public affairs are nearly all progressive in thought and favour the same ideas more or less. So that the danger is not altogether imaginary that on most questions coming up before them they are apt to seize the same points and neglect the same points. When to this consideration is added the great variety of interests and communities and the wide disparity of the education and upbringing of different classes, the *a priori* case for another Chamber seems strong. It cannot pass the wit of Indian statesmen to devise a second House of legislature composed, either entirely or as to a majority, of members elected for a longer term of years than the first House and by electorates constituted on different principles, so that there would be a strong probability of its views supplementing on important matters the views taken elsewhere. The recent Irish Home Rule Act probably utilises the experience of the world in this respect, and Mr. Redmond who has no reason to love the English House of Lords, spoke of the Act as follows in Parliament: "Viewing the Bill as a "whole, I say here—and I speak for my colleagues "on these benches—that this is a great measure and "a measure adequate to carry out the objects of its "promoters. It is a great measure and we welcome "it." It sets up a second House under the name of the Senate. Its constitution and relations to the other House are summarised below: "The Irish "Senate shall consist of forty senators, the first to be "nominated by the Lord Lieutenant on the advice of the "Executive Committee. The term of office of senators "shall be eight years, and shall not be affected by a "dissolution; one fourth to retire every second year "and their seats to be filled by new nomination. Bills "appropriating revenue or money or imposing taxation "shall originate only in the Irish House of Commons, "which shall not adopt or pass any resolution, address "or Bill for the appropriation for any purpose of any "part of the public revenue of Ireland or of any tax, "except in pursuance of a recommendation from the "Lord Lieutenant. The Irish Senate may not reject "any Bill which deals only with the imposition of "taxation or appropriation of revenue or money, and "may not amend any Bill so far as the Bill imposes "taxation or appropriates revenue or money, or so as "to increase any proposed burden on the people. Any "Bill which appropriates revenue or money for the "ordinary annual services of the Irish Government "shall deal only with that appropriation. In the "event of continued disagreement between the two "Irish Houses, a joint sitting may be convened and "the matter in dispute settled by a joint vote." In view, however, of the almost perfect unanimity of Indian opinion against the idea, it is needless to say more on the subject. A few valuable opinions, however, will be given on the general question of a second Chamber.

John Stuart Mill; "A majority in a single as-"sembly, when it has assumed a permanent character "—when composed of the same persons habitually "acting together, and always assured of victory in "their own House—easily becomes despotic and over-"weening, if released from the necessity of consider-"ing whether its acts will be concurred in by another "constituted authority. The same reason which in-"duced the Romans to have two consuls, makes it "desirable there should be two chambers, that neither "of them may be exposed to the corrupting influence "of undivided power, even for the space of a single "year." Walter Bagehot: "With a perfect Lower "House it is certain that an Upper House would be "scarcely of any value. If we had an ideal House of "Commons perfectly representing the nation, always "moderate, never passionate, abounding in men of "leisure, never omitting the slow and steady forms "necessary for good consideration, it is certain that "we should not need a higher chamber. The work "would be done so well that we should not want any "one to look over or revise it. And whatever is un-"necessary in government, is pernicious. . . . But "though beside an ideal House of Commons the Lords "would be unnecessary, and therefore pernicious, "beside the actual House a revising and leisured "legislature is extremely useful, if not quite neces-"sary." W. E. H. Lecky: "Of all the forms of govern-"ment that are possible among mankind I do not "know any which is likely to be worse than the "government of a single democratic Chamber." Henry Sidgwick: "The main end for which a Senate "is constructed (is) that all legislative measures may "receive a second consideration by a body different "in character from the primary representative as-"sembly, and if possible superior or supplementary "in intellectual qualifications." Alphaeus Todd: "In

"Colonies entrusted with the powers of local self-"government... a second chamber is a necessary "institution. . . . It is a counterpoise to democratic "ascendency in the popular and most powerful as-"sembly, it affords some protection against hasty ill-"considered legislation and action, and serves to "elicit the sober second thought of the people, in "contradistinction to the impulsive first thought of "the Lower House." Alexander Hamilton: "There "is reason to expect that this branch (of the legis-"lature) will usually be composed with peculiar care "and judgment; that (the Senators) ... will be less apt "to be tainted by the spirit of faction, and more out "of the reach of those occasional ill-humours or tem-"porary prejudices and propensities which in smaller "societies frequently contaminate the public delibera-"tions, beget injustice and oppression towards a part "of the community, and engender schemes which, "though they gratify a momentary inclination or "desire, terminate in general distress, dissatisfaction, "and disgust." Sir Henry Maine: "What, then, is "expected from a well constituted second Chamber is "not a rival infallibility, but an additional security. "It is hardly too much to say that, in this view, al-"most any second Chamber is better than none." The Abbé Siéyés: "If a second chamber dissents from the "first, it is mischievous; if it agrees with it, it is "superfluous." Goldwin Smith: "To construct a body "which, without claiming a co-ordinate authority, "shall act as a court of legislative revision, and as "the sober second thought of the community, is prac-"tically beyond the power of the political architect. "He must try to ensure sobriety where he places "power. To suppose that power will allow itself on "important matters to be controlled by impotence is "vain."

PLACE IN RECONSTRUCTED EMPIRE ?

Our Anglo-Indian brethren are naturally more interested in the problem of India's place in the future Empire of Greater Britain than in that of her internal autonomy, and they will smile at our defective sense of proportion in neglecting a larger for a smaller subject. The scheme before us has only one reference to the subject, laying down the general requirement that in the reconstruction of the empire India should be placed on the same footing as the Dominions. This would follow almost as a corollary from the self-governing status which, as has been already stated, must be conceded before the imperial problem is taken up. It will certainly not suit Anglo-Indians. Their political superiority and the economic lead that follows from it are already secured to them. Internal autonomy will first weaken and finally efface both. Besides, at the Imperial Conference or the Convention that may be summoned for discussing the larger problems of empire, they would be precluded from claiming to be the best, if not the only, representatives of India. No wonder their notion of the relative urgency and importance of the two allied questions is so different from that of Indians. There is every reason to fear that, if India were not to be represented by her own natural leaders in the future imperial organization, her true economic and other interests would not receive adequate protection. Why, even the Government of India, being that of a Dependency, had to go to the wall in the contest with the Government of South Africa, although they had an overwhelmingly just cause. Some

Dominion writers recognize the justice or expediency, it does not matter which, of giving the people of India, as distinguished from the Government or the European community temporarily resident here, some place in the future Imperial Parliament of Greater Britain. But they make a sharp distinction between the educated Indians who have adopted western ways of thought and the bulk of the population who are still illiterate and, according to western notions, unfit to take any part in public affairs. Mr. Curtis, whose book is for the hour the political Bible of the Anglo-Indian community, lays down the proposition that "in the World-Commonwealth the function of government is reserved to the European minority, for the unanswerable reason that for the present this portion of its citizens is alone capable of the task." He admits, however, there are a handful of public men standing on an equal footing with Europeans and fit to supply cabinets and parliaments, who now enjoy the power of influencing the Government of India by being admitted to its legislature. Their claim to be consulted in imperial affairs he concedes to be reasonable, though the precise way in which he would meet the claim is to be expounded in a future book. Mr. Worsfold has evolved the outline of a scheme for the constitution of an Imperial Senate and an Imperial House of Representatives in which he tries, according to his measure, to do justice to the coloured races under the sway of the British Crown. He divides the Empire into white states and coloured states. In both Chambers of the Empire the coloured states and the coloured races, although they are immensely superior in numbers, are to have one-fourth representation. The members of the Senate may be elected by the white states, but must be nominated in the case of the coloured states by their Governments. The persons so nominated may belong to the white or the coloured races. The coloured men who may be elected to either chamber must have been admitted to what is known as the white franchise, *i.e.*, the power to take part in elections by white constituencies on equal terms with white persons. For his idea is that the representation of the coloured races even in coloured states must be by separate electorates of their own. The white franchise is to be conferred on proof before a court of one of a number of qualifications: "(*a*) the "holding of any office of a certain class under the Uni- "on or a State Government; (*b*) the possession of a "degree granted by a recognised university; (*c*)member- "ship of a learned profession; (*d*) the holding of a "commercial position of importance; (*e*) the possession "of moveable or immoveable property; and (*f*) the per- "formance of any service of benefit to the community "as a whole." Of the one-fourth representation allowed to the coloured states India gets 60 per cent., the exact figures of Mr. Worsfold being 30 out of a total of 200 in the Senate and 65 out of a total of 400 in the House of Representatives. Representation proportionate to population is out of the question, for then India would get three-fourths and no Ministry can escape dependence on the Indian vote. In other words, "India would rule the Empire." Besides, the vast majority of the Indian peoples cannot exercise the vote intelligently. So Mr. Worsfold sums up: "The object to be attained is therefore to find an "electoral system which will give the real people of "India an effective representation in the Lower House "of the Central Legislature, *without endangering the control of European States over it or otherwise lowering its efficiency as the chief organ of Imperial administration.*" (The italics are ours.) So we can now understand the difficulty of those who have to frame a constitution for the Empire. To admit India is to enthrone her; to exclude her is iniquitous. So the compromise is to cripple her first and then to admit her. The Mahomedans of India, being in a small minority, want and are allowed excessive representation. The Indians in the Empire, being in an overwhelming majority, are to be dragged into a Federation with a greatly reduced representation. What a diversity of principles in one political organization! India is the difficulty, the Gordian knot which can only be cut. She must suffer for her size and importance and value to the empire. It is not wise to bite off more than you can chew. Lord Milner is a strong, brave man. He frankly gives the go-by to justice or equality. This is how he would give the franchise to the black and the power to the white "I never can see why the property and education tests need be identical for black and white. I should deliberately and quite frankly make them *higher* for the black, and I am prepared to justify this. But whatever the standard proposed, let there be some standard the attainment of which will relieve the coloured man, of whatever race, from all *legal* disadvantages, as compared with the white." (Quoted by Mr. Worsfold.) There are many eminent men, both in England and the Dominions, whose imagination has been captivated by the idea of Imperial Federation. But there are some men whose opinion is also entitled to weight who think it unwise and impracticable. Most Indian leaders, if they had a voice, would oppose the ideal. Their belief is that, if she is not to have self-government, India is now in safer hands than she would be in the new regime.

AN INCONSISTENCY

The scheme is marred in the eyes of some critics by an inconsistency. Demanding complete financial autonomy, inclusive of the right to regulate tariffs, the authors of the scheme propose to leave all military and naval expenditure as heretofore in the hands of the executive government, without control by the legislature. The statement is true. In fact, the advocates of Home Rule for India do not touch the question of the defence of India, thus placing her on a lower level than the Dominions, which in recent years have organized an army and a navy of their own, over which they retain full control. Furthermore, the jurisdiction over questions connected with the army which the Legislative Council of the Viceroy now enjoys would seem to be surrendered in this scheme. Logic and consistency, however, are not to be expected in matters where the the necessity of compromise is supreme. No principle can be pushed to its full conclusion without checks and safeguards. So long as resolutions brought forward by Additional Members had no chance of being passed except with the consent of Government and, even when so passed, had only the force of recommendations, it could not much matter even if army questions came within the scope of the Council. But the position becomes different under a scheme which creates an autonomous legislature with a majority of elected members. The Imperial authorities would decline to look at the scheme unless it provided guarantees not only of the safety of the country, but of the maintenance of its connection with the British Empire. The claim may be made in all sincerity that the authors of the scheme, in making this serious deduction from financial autonomy, have given conclusive evidence of their loyalty to the British Sovereign and of their belief that within the British Empire the highest ideals of Indian patriots could be realized. In fact, a suggestion was made while the scheme was under discussion that the exclusion of the military from the control of the Legislative Council should be only for a certain number of years but the Committee of the Congress rejected it without hesitation.

ELECTED EXECUTIVE

The provision for the Indian half of the Executive Council being elected has met with a certain amount of criticism. It is true there is comparatively small precedent for Ministries being chosen by election. It is done in Switzerland and in the case of the Provincial Committees of South Africa. The idea has often been suggested in Australia, but has never been adopted. One objection to the plan is that it will not fit in well with a parliamentary system of government, where ministers have to resign if defeated on any important issue. Our scheme, however, does not purport to create a parliamentary plan of government. The constitutional objection then does not apply here. There is more force in another objection—that by the process of election you cannot always get the most competent men available; on the contrary the qualities that conduce to success at election are by no means the qualities that conduce to success in office. But what is the alternative to election? Nomination by the Viceroy. He may select his ministers either from officials or from non-officials. Now public opinion in India is strong against the appointment of officials to the Executive Council of the Government of India. This is a principle which cannot be compromised except for special reasons. If the choice is to be made from non-officials, can any Viceroy be trusted to possess the necessary knowledge of the men available in the different provinces? The arts by which exalted officials may be taken in are not less degrading than the well-known arts of canvassing by which the votes of electors are secured. The opportunities of familiar intercourse and conversation with Indian gentlemen of standing that the Viceroy has are so few that he cannot ordinarly be expected to have the means of ascertaining the real character and reputation that a candidate possesses in his community. On the contrary, if the Viceroy did know of any man of outstanding merit, he would in all probability appoint him; but then the same man would in all probability come out top in an election as well. From this point of view there is not much to choose between the methods. The real danger is the large amount of canvassing and log-rolling which the prospect of two prize-posts will bring about, with the consequent demoralization of the electorate. There is no effective remedy short of an impossibly high code of honour. The gentlemen responsible for the scheme were carried away by two considerations, first, the fear based on same amount of experience that incompetence and sycophancy will not be discounted by the Viceroy when united to aristocratic birth; secondly, the need of securing, in the absence of the power of displacing a ministry, that at least one half of it should be presumably *en rapport* with the Legislative Council. Still it is not one of the strongest points of the scheme and, if it does not yield good results, we shall not be without the means of changing it.

EDUCATED OLIGARCHY

The next objection to be noticed is that, if the scheme came into operation, it would establish the reign of the few who are educated over the many who are uneducated, we should have an oligarchy of a few hundred thousands controlling the destinies of vast millions. You reply that, taking numbers only into consideration, the change will be a big step towords popular government, as the present ruling class does not exceed a few thousands. "But we have knowledge," say they, "of rural life and of the dumb millions, which you, educated gentry dwelling in towns, cannot and do not care to acquire." "It is not so," we rejoin; "the gulf of antipathy and contempt between educated and uneducated is a fable by which you deceive yourselves. The educated come mostly from villages and keep in constant touch with village life. In fact, the most notorious evil of the present administration is that it is run by people who come from over the sea, never learn the vernaculars sufficiently well for ordinary conversation and depend throughout their service on interpreters. Besides, they maintain an attitude of proud exclusiveness which differs in kind and manner of display from the ancient arrogance of the Brahman, but is a far more effectual barrier to sympathy and mutual trust; in fact it is now an article of creed with them that India and Indians are unfathomable mysteries and that, the longer one remains in the country, the more convinced one becomes of the impossibility of ever understanding its people and their nature and modes of thought and life." "But the lower classes look to us for protection, they remember the old misrule and tyranny from which we rescued them, and will not consent to the transfer of power from us to you, their social oppressors for ages." "Our history, like the history of other peoples, shows periods of good rule and bad rule, of social well-being and social misery, of progress and decay. When you came you found us in one of our unfortunate phases, disorder and the breaking up of an empire met your eyes and helped the establishment of your dominion. The oppression of the lower by the upper classes is nothing peculiar to the East. Before the dawn of the modern humanitarian age, the annals of Europe were disfigured by similar abuses and tyranny. Plato long ago said that in every city there were two cities, that of the rich and that of the poor. To-day, even in the most liberally governed countries, the peasants and the labourers may be heard to denounce the learned folly and the selfishness of those that make the laws and work them for their own benefit, while all the time professing to help and relieve the masses. Ideas of social amelioration and service and higher standards of government have been learned by the educated men in India, and as they have incomparably greater interest in the prosperity of the country and far more knowledge and sympathy to inspire their efforts, there is no danger of a revival of the old days of caste domination and heartless tyranny. The new oligarchy then will be at least as good as the present." One doubts whether this ancient fiction about the protection of the masses is believed any more even by those in whose interest it is kept alive. Is it the indigenous

Short or the oversea Codlin who opposes the spread of education among the people and uses their illiteracy as an argument for opposing political advance? Is it the indigenous Short or the oversea Codlin who defends the pernicious excise policy of the Government on the ground that every man must have his tastes, and likewise approves of the raising of the State demand on land at every resettlement on the ground among others that money left in the ryot's hands goes to the drink shop? Who allows the country to be flooded with cheap free trade goods and refuses to foster the industries of the people in the only way in which other countries, including Great Britain and her colonies, have fostered theirs? Who was responsible for the currency legislation of a few years ago, which, but for some fortuitous happenings which told in his favour, might have hit the poor agriculturist hard, while relieving the Government of the exchange difficulty in paying off the heavy Home charges? Who at the same time gave the European services the exchange compensation allowance in cynical disregard of the tax-payer's interests? Who to-day, when extravagance is treason and luxuries of every kind are denounced as crimes, keeps up the exodus to the hills for half the year and sanctions extra allowances to Civilian officers for promotion delayed, while at the same time cutting down expenditure on education? Who is going to defend the interests of the voiceless and voteless tax-payer, when in consequence of the report of the Public Services Commission the organised and well-paid Services will drive the Government of India mad with all sorts of claims for increased emoluments? The unfortunate Indian Short, in a hopeless minority in the Council, must set up a piteous wail, which, however, will be drowned in the noise of Codlin's trumpet announcing to an astounded world his protection of of the Indian masses against their own heartless countrymen.

It is certainly not political wisdom to keep the educated classes out of their own on the overdrawn plea that the European must continue to play Providence to the masses of India. Their ambition, to put it no higher, is not a vice to be condemned and put down. It is the witness of the eternal principle of progress implanted in man, coloured as well as colourless, and those that contemn it contemn the noblest part of themselves. Lord Durham put the matter none too strongly when he wrote: "As long as personal ambi-"tion is inherent in human nature, and as long as "the morality of every free and civilized community "encourages its aspirations, it is one great business "of a wise Government to provide for its legitimate "development. If, as it is commonly asserted, the "disorders of these colonies have in great measure, "been fomented by the influence of designing and "ambitious individuals, this evil will best be remedied "by allowing such a scope for the desires of such "men as shall direct their ambition into the legitimate "channel of furthering, and not of thwarting, their "Government. By creating high prizes in a general "and responsible Government, we shall immeditely "afford the means of pacifying the turbulent am-"bitions, and of employing in worthy and noble "occupations the talents which now are only exerted "to foment disorder. We must remove from these "colonies the cause to which the sagacity of Adam "Smith traced the alienation of the provinces which "now form the United States: we must provide some "scope for what he calls 'the importance' of the lead- "ing men in the colony, beyond what he forcibly "terms the present 'petty prizes of the paltry raffle "of colonial faction'." Mr. Curtis too deprecates the talent of educated and competent men being allowed to run to waste. "Citizens who have actually deve- "loped the capacity for government will tend to lose "it unless it is used to the full. Their knowledge and "sense of responsibility will not only be wasted, but "will languish for want of exercise. They will not "be brought into touch with the ultimate facts of "political decisions in which they themselves have "shared. They will become a weakness instead of a "strength to the commonwealth. The state positive- "ly suffers from excluding from political responsi- "bility any class of citizens who have clearly deve- "loped a knowledge and sense of duty sufficient for "the task. There is always room, therefore, for the "further extension of responsible government, and "there is always the necessity for it. More men can "be made more free by being made more responsible "for the conduct of public affairs, and by being put "in a position in which, while they suffer for mis- "takes, they share in the power of correcting them."

THE MARTIAL RACES WILL RISE

The last objection that we shall deal with in this section is that the martial races, believing that the Government of the land has passed into weak hands when it passed into Indian hands, will raise the standard of revolt and shake the new regime at the very start. In the first place, this cannot be true of either the Mahomedans, the Sikhs, or the Marathas, who have drunk deep from the fountain of patriotism.

In the second place, when service in the army is thrown open to all who are physically fit and promotion is within the reach of all who are worthy, irrespective of race or colour, the distinction between martial and unmartial people will disappear in the course of a generation. But the real answer to this objection is that it would apply only to a scheme which sought to take India out of the British Empire and completely eliminated the strong arm of the British from Indian affairs. Our critics may choose for their own alarmist purposes to misrepresent the effect of our proposals or the motive that underlies them. But, as a great man once said, "You may fool some of the people all the time and all the people some of the time, but not all the people all the time." The scheme has for its aim and purpose the continued maintenance of British supremacy in India and the reconciliation of her peoples to the suzerainty of the British empire, which has done them incalculable good, giving them hope of a nationhood that they had lost or never possessed, and admitting them to a share of the noblest inheritance of modern civilization, *viz.*, democratic freedom. The sentiment of devotion to the British Commowealth conveyed in the following passage from Mr. Curtis, omitting the phrase which refers to the sense of kinship, will find a heartfelt echo in the bosoms of most political leaders of India: "Their devotion to it, how-"ever consecrated by a sense of kinship, is finally "rooted in the belief that the Commonwealth is the "greatest institution in the world for enabling men to "realize the duty of governing themselves. It is "mainly because they know that it stands for the "cause of self-government, and that with its destruc-"tion that cause would languish, that they find "themselves ready to devote their lives and their "wealth to keep it inviolable." The scheme provides for the Viceroy and the heads of Provincial Governments being appointed by the Crown direct. Half the members of the Executive Councils will under it be Europeans, and the Indian Civil Service will continue for many years yet to have a preponderant British element. The case will be nearly the same with the police. The bulk of the commercial interests will also be in European hands. Above all, the entire control of the Military is, of purpose to afford the necessary guarantee, vested in the Viceroy's hands. It is difficult to see what there is in these conditions to make the martial races believe that the pressure that keeps them down is removed and they can work their lawless will on the defenceless people. The educated Indian knows better than to grasp the reins of power if he thought that he could hold them only for a brief day.

WILL ENGLISHMEN RENOUNCE POWER?

THEIR MISSION IN INDIA

Many who grant the essential justness of the foregoing reasoning may still feel that due account has not been taken of the human element in the problem. Is it to be expected that the Anglo-Saxon, who has come to believe that his special mission is to dominate or, as he prefers to call it, to elevate the weaker races of the world, will renounce the power that has come into his hands? England is truly the home of freedom, but Mill said that all men love power more than liberty. The saying has peculiar force if the power is yours and the liberty is other men's. This is true of most individuals, but there are occasions of moral fervour when it is not true of some high-souled men and women. And there are periods in the history even of aggressive nations when it has not been true of them collectively. In this sense a nation may be nobler than the individual, its genius higher than the tendency of the average citizen. A broad survey of the history of England leaves the impression that, despite great lapses, the spirit of her civilization is a love of free institutions for all. The Government of England, moving within the restraints imposed by diplomacy and traditional policy, has not always championed the cause of freedom. But the great heart of England has ever beaten in sympathy with struggling peoples, whether it be in revolted America, revolutionary France, Italy, Greece or Belgium. Slavery, which was a great blot on human civilization till recently and involved ancient empires in moral ruin, was abolished first in England. And her shining example has spread over the civilized world. Serfdom and contract labour, which are modified forms of slavery, have nearly ceased to exist in the British Empire, and the knell of indentured labour in India has been sounded. Political subordination remains, but the conscience of England no longer justifies it in its nakedness, but as a necessary preparation of unfit communities for liberty. Often alas! some of her representatives call liberty a shibboleth, and some of her proconsuls in the east have denied her mission and committed wanton aggressions in the name of empire. But nemesis has followed close upon their heels and sooner or later their misdeeds have been converted into benefactions. Malcolm and Elphinstone are only two of a large number of high-souled British administrators who dreamed of an India which should no longer need the support of England. The enunciation of a noble and humane policy may occasionally be mixed with a certain amount of cant, but it has a way of becoming imbedded in political thought and purifying the springs of political action. It has been said that evolution is a spiral movement, backward and forward, but in the long run more forward than backward. So is it with British rule in India. A few years ago we seemed to be swept back by a mighty tide of reaction. The officials of the time seemed deliberately to forswear the beneficence and magnanimity of their predecessors. An exponent of this phase of political thought, approved and belauded by officials themselves, M. Joseph Chailley, writes: "It was "so at one time, in the era of Malcolm and "Mountstuart Elphinstone (about 1830), and even "after the mutiny, when the British considered their "mission in India as being to educate the people, to "make a nation of them, and to prepare them for the "task of self-government. That task accomplished, "in the course of a century or two, they would retire, "leaving it to its own destinies, a glorious child of their "genius. But this conception is not now that of the "generality of Englishmen, though it has still some "few adherents—Sir Henry Cotton, for instance, who "presided over the National Congress of 1904. "British opinion, whether in India or the mother "country, would now no longer consider a policy of "evacuation; the ties which bind India to England "are too strong. India is one of the main pillars "upon which the grandeur of the British Empire "rests; and England will not willingly let her go." "Had England taken as her motto, 'India for the "Indians,' had she continued, following the ideas of "Elphinstone and Malcolm, to consider her rule as tem-"porary, she might, without inconsistency, grant "to the national party gradual and increasing con-"cessions, which in time would give entire autonomy "to the Indians. But that is not now her aim. She "rules India, and intends to go on ruling it. She has "against her a Hindu minority; for her, other "minorities—Mussalmans, Buddhists and Parsis—"and the great mass of the Hindu population. She "is ready to bestow on the national party honours "and posts in increasing numbers, but she will make "no compromise in the matter of principle. She will "keep the command and direction of the vessel, and "her Government will remain as despotic as cir-"cumstances will permit. Macaulay said in 1835: "'We know that India cannot have a free government, "but she can have the next best thing, a strong and "impartial despotism.' Seventy years later, Sir "Edward Baker, the late Indian Finance Minister, "took up practically the same position. India is and "must remain, he said, a portion of the British Em-"pire and must in the last resort be subject to the "control of the British Government. Complete auto-"nomy would be inadmissible as regards internal ad-"ministration; still more so as regards military mat-"ters and external policy. Any projects of radical "reform would be sheltered (shattered?) against this "firm decision, which can only be overcome by "force." But this is treason to God's law, which is love and beneficence. It could not prevail for ever, and Malcolm and Elphinstone must be vindicated. The better mind of England has reasserted itself in the direction of Indian policy and is aptly expressed by Sir Theodore Morison in this passage: "In the background of every Englishman's mind "is probably to be found the conviction that it is "our duty so to govern India that she may one day "be able to govern herself, and as an autonomous "unit take her place in the great confederation of "the British Empire. This is the ultimate justifica-"tion of our Asiatic dominion, and a statesman who "ventured to advocate the alternative policy that "India should be kept in a state of perpetual vassal-"age, as the milch cow of England, would be hooted "from public life."

BLOOD TIES NOT ESSENTIAL

If hope is immortal, so unfortunately seems doubt. The pessimist has his own reading of history. The British, he fears, have granted freedom only to people of their own blood. The examples of the French Canadians and the Boers fail to convince him. In both cases there were British people to whom responsible government had to be given, and care was taken that they had the balance of political power in their hands. The Filipinos, who might be a clear case in point, are unfortunately outside the British mpire. Ireland's fate still hangs in the balance; even there the Ulster Protesants, who are mainly British, must be excluded from Home Rule or conciliated by adequate guarantees. History then has no exact parallel to comfort us. But we have England's pledge and, in spite of our pessimistic friend, we are in the line of progress. Why may it not be our good fortune to be, within this world-wide empire, the first non-British people to obtain self-government by peaceful and constitutional methods only? As Mr. Gokhale once said, the history of the world is not finished; many chapters have yet to be added to it. One bright chapter under the grace of God may be the joint contribution of England and India. M. Chailley writes for a class of Anglo-Indians who habitually represent the political movement in India as aimed at the expulsion of the British and the complete severance of the country from the British empire. This aim did not actuate any but a small knot of revolutionaries and that for a time. The furious denunciation, therefore, of M. Chailley and his friends leaves our withers unwrung. We ask that the Britisher's privileged position in India should cease, that in our own country and indeed throughout the British empire we should be no wise inferior, by reason merely of race, birth, colour, or religion, to any class of His Imperial Majesty's subjects, and that we should be allowed hereafter, Dominion-fashion and in fulfilment of solemn pledges, to regulate the internal affairs of our motherland. No more humiliating restrictions for the individual, no more economic subservience for the community, no more political subordination except as to imperial interests and the Crown's prerogatives. Why does the demand of such an elementary principle of modern civilization as the absolute equality of all before the law bring violent imprecations on our heads? It is on record that when the little garrison of Arcot ran short of provisions, Clive's sepoys said to his soldiers, "You eat the rice, we'll drink the *conjee.*" Surely the good souls did not think at the time that it should be "rice to you and *conjee* to us" for ever. No; this question, once raised, must be set at rest, or it will come up again and again. Unsettled problems, as Burke said once, have no consideration for the repose of nations. Hope is for man, not men; there is no monopoly in freedom. Bright, speaking of Ireland, was led by the logic of his thought to widen it out: "I have never maintained that Irishmen are not "at liberty to ask for and, if they could accomplish "it, to obtain the repeal of the Union. I say we have "no right whatever to insist on a Union between "Ireland and Great Britain upon our terms only. I "am one of those who admit, as every sensible man "must admit, that an Act which the Parliament of the "United Kingdom has passed, the Parliament of the "United Kingdom can repeal; and further, I am will-"ing to admit that everybody in England allows, "with regard to every foreign country, that any "nation, believing it to be its interest, has a right both "to ask for and to strive for national independence." Similarly, Lord Durham, in writing of Canada, was unconsciously pleading for other peoples as well. Sir Charles Lucas in an eloquent passage draws out the implications of the noble lord's doctrine. "To all times and to all sorts and conditions of "men he has preached the doctrine that for peoples, "as for individuals, the one thing worth living for is "to make, not to destroy; to build up not to pull "down; to unite small disjointed elements into a "single whole; to reject absolutely and always the "doctrine of *divide et impera*, because it is a sign of "weakness, not of strength; to be strong and fear not; "to speak unto the peoples of the earth that they go "forward. In this constructiveness, which is em-"bodied in all parts of the report, he has, beyond any "other man, illustrated in writing the genius of the "English race, the element which in the British Em-"pire is common alike to the sphere of settlement "and to the sphere of rule." The idealists of Europe, here is Lord Bryce's word for it, have dreamed of happiness for all people alike flowing from the establishment of free institutions. "But from 1830 to "1870 the general attitude of most of the powerful in-"tellects and nearly all the finest characters among the "thinkers and writers of Europe was a hopeful one, ex-"pecting immense gains to human progress and human "happiness from the establishment of free institu-"tions. These expectations have been in so far realised "that the condition of all the countries where such in-"stitutions now exist shows a marked improvement in "the condition of the masses of the people, an improve-"ment due not merely to the advance of science and "consequent diffusion of comfort, but also to a juster "and more humane legislation. Nobody denies that our "world of to-day is a better world for the common man. "Few deny that this is largely due to better political "institutions. A striking evidence of this general "conviction is to be found in the efforts which Japan "and Russia have made, which Persia and the Turks "are beginning to make, for the establishment of parlia-"mentary institutions. Even in China these have "been talked of: *De conducendo loquitur iam rhetore "thule.*"

CONCLUSION

OUR DUTY

Everywhere men are asking one another: "What will come of it all?" They would fain penetrate the veil that hides the future. The result depends on a number of more or less incalculable factors, but one of these, and not a negligible one, is the earnestness and strength of the effort made by the people of India. Though it may not be flattering to our vanity, it must be acknowledged that we have not yet mastered the art of political agitation. The machinery of government in Great Britain is moved by public opinion. Those that are keen on getting anything done have to secure its support. This is got up by a persistent campaign of writing in newspapers, lectures, deputations, and other demonstrations, more or less noisy. Some movements have organs of their own and a corps of paid agents. The interest of members of Parliament, front bench men preferably, has to be obtained if the Cabinet has to take action. When the Colonies obtained Parliamentary legislation for responsible government and other great objects, they sent over deputations, and some members thereof stayed in London for long periods. When the Bills were drafting, they must have had several private interviews with men of consequence. In India the imperative need of this work is not sufficiently recognized. Our difficulty in this respect is specially great, because we have to contend against the influence of the reactionary members of the Government of India, the India Office, the great bulk of retired Anglo-Indians and the numerous conservative organs of the press. Our exertions must therefore be strenuous and unceasing, our sacrifices heavy in proportion. Nor must work in India be neglected. In many ways it is not less, but more, important than agitation in England. When the end of the war is in sight, numbers of enthusiastic workers must carry the gospel of self-government for India under the British flag nto every nook and corner of the land, pamphlets and leaflets, besides articles in the press, must rain ion the country in English and in the vernaculars, and memorials, preferably translations of one and the same original, signed by tens of thousands of people must be got ready for transmission to the authorities. Representatives of Indian opinion, men of light and leading in every locality, all who have any opportunities of conversation with officials, must not shrink, when asked, from proclaiming their whole-hearted adherence to the Congress scheme. It should not be possible for any officer in any corner to report to Government, confidentially or otherwise, that he did not hear much of the self-government movement in his jurisdiction. Despite all these manifestations of popular enthusiasm, it is probable that the fulfilment of our aspiration will be long in coming. Disappointments and discouragements, mockery and abuse may assail us at every turn. Threat and persecution may be the portion of some of the patriots actively engaged in the cause. Nothing, however, should be allowed to turn us aside from our undertaking. There will arise frequent occasion for change of plan, increased vigilance, more man-power. But occasion for despair there cannot be. God's grace must rest on all righteous causes. No obstacle can stand before a nation's will. We have only to teach the nation to form this will, and all can help in this work.

TAKE OCCASION BY THE HAND

The truth will bear repetition that in British polity great changes may be brought about by the sole means of constitutional agitation. It is the boast of English historians that by timely concessions and adjustments their statesmen have as a rule averted violence and revolution. Let our workers, young and old, remember always that a good cause does not need to be served by bad means. We shall perhaps have provocation now and then from underlings; a small man, dressed up in a little brief authority, may occasionally do a stupid thing. The exuberant imagination with which we have been credited should enable us to make due allowance for the extreme difficulty of the European's position in India. A few thousands among vast millions, they have excuse if in times of political excitement they yield to unjust suspicion and act in panic. Our movement will not lose but gain in the end by being conducted with restraint and dignity. If violence there must be, let it be what others inflict on us; if suffering, let it be what we bear; if sacrifice, let it be what we make, not what we exact. The time is full of hard problems for British statesmen. They can attend to none which are not urgent and cannot by any possibility be put off. Even in ordinary times, if a question has not sufficient momentum of public opinion or even clamour behind it, other questions will take precedence. The habit of politicians in England is to judge the urgency of a matter by the noise it has made and by the earnestness of the men that champion it. In this struggle for attention it often happens that a movement wins on account of the trouble that it has caused the administration and the disorderly manifestations it has made of its strength and intensity. It must be admitted that we in India are not good at attracting the notice of the authorities and guardians of the public peace in these ways. We lie under a peculiar disadvantage in that even youthful indiscretion is branded by inconsiderate authorities as a symptom of sedition or disloyalty. Tests of a different kind must therefore be applied to our movements. *The Times of India* the other day pleaded for a complete change in the mode of action of British ministers. It admonished them for waiting till they *must* act. To some extent it is a condition imposed by the congestion of Parliamentary work, but it is also the inevitable result of democracy or government by the people. "Yet under the British system Mr. Asquith has "had to draw his whole inspiration from the country "instead of leading and influencing the country; one "result is that in all major preparations the Empire "has had to wait until the good sense and patriotism "of the people have gathered sufficient momentum to "drive the Government to action. It does not require "much mental effort to see at what a disadvantage "this places the British Empire when at death "grips with a Government that really governs— "which with a vast organised body of expert know-"ledge at its disposal is able to act in advance of "public opinion without waiting until the mass of "people, who with their imperfect knowledge neces-"sarily see things more slowly, have made up their "minds that action shall be taken." To Indians who are peace-loving, full of trust in the authorities and accustomed to leave the initiative to them, the change of attitude here recommended will be a blessing. The old ideal of the good and wise king who went about among his people in search of wrong and suffering that he may give redress before the tear was shed or the curse spoken still holds our imagination. It cannot be a sound polity where the normal practice is to meet a situation only when it has developed undesirable symptoms.

APPENDIX I

MEMORANDUM OF "THE NINETEEN"

MEMORANDUM SUBMITTED BY ELECTED MEMBERS OF THE IMPERIAL LEGISLATIVE COUNCIL

The following is the full text of the Memorandum submitted to the Viceroy by nineteen elected additional members of the Imperial Legislative Council with regard to "post-war reforms" in India:—

There is no doubt that the termination of the war will see a great advance in the ideals of government all over the civilised world and especially in the British Empire, which entered into the struggle in defence of the liberties of weak and small nationalities and is pouring forth its richest blood and treasure in upholding the cause of justice and humanity in the international relations of the world. India has borne her part in this struggle and cannot remain unaffected by the new spirit of change for a better state of things. Expectations have been raised in this country and hopes held out that, after the war, the problems of Indian administration will be looked at from a new angle of vision.

The Uncompleted Work of 1909

The people of India have good reasons to be grateful to England for the great progress in her material resources and the widening of her intellectual and political outlook under British rule, and for the steady, if slow, advance in her national life commencing with the Charter Act of India of 1833. Up to 1909, the Government of India was conducted by a bureaucracy almost entirely non-Indian in its composition and not responsible to the people of India. The reforms of 1909 for the first time introduced an Indian element in the direction of affairs in the administration of India. This element was of a very limited character. The Indian people accepted it as an indication on the part of the Government of a desire to admit the Indians into the inner counsels of the Indian Empire.

So far as the Legislative Councils are concerned, the numbers of non-official members were merely enlarged with increased facilities for debate and interpellation. The Supreme

Legislative Council retained an absolute official majority, and in the Provincial Legislative Councils, where a non-official mojority was allowed, such majority included nominated members and the European representatives. In measures largely affecting the people, whether of legislation or taxation, by which Europeans were not directly affected, the European members would naturally support the Government and the nominated members, being nominees of Government, would be inclined to take the same side. Past experience has shown that this has actually happened on various occasions. The non-official majorities, therefore, in the Provincial Councils have proved largely illusory and give no real power to the representatives of the people. The Legislative Councils, whether Supreme or Provincial, are at present nothing but advisory bodies without any power of effective control over the Government, Imperial or Provincial. The people or their representatives are practically as little associated with the real government of the country as they were before the reforms, except for the introduction of the Indian element in the Executive Councils, where again the nomination rests entirely wlth the Government, the people having no voice in the selection of the Indian members.

The object which the Government had in view in introducing the reforms of 1909 was, as expressed by the Prime Minister in his speech in the House of Commons on the second reading of the Indian Councils Bill (April 1, 1909), that "it was most desirable in the circumstances to give to the people of India the feeling that these Legislative Councils are not mere automatons the wires of which are pulled by the official hierarchy." This object, it is submitted, has not been attained.

Other Grave Disabilities

Apart from this question of the constitution of the Legislative and Executive Councils, the people labour under certain grave disabilities, which not only prevent the utilisation, but also lead to the wastage, of what is best in them, and are positively derogatory to their sense of nationl self-respect. The Arms Act, which excludes from its operation Europeans and Anglo-Indians and applies only to the pure natives of the country, the disqualification of Indians for forming or joining Volunteer corps, and their exclusion from the commissioned ranks of the army, are disabilities which are looked upon with an irritating sense of racial differentiation. It would be bad enough if these were mere disabilities. Restrictions aud prohibitions regarding the possession and use of arms have tended to emasculate the civil population in India and expose them to serious danger. The position of Indians in India is practically this, that they have no real part or share in the direction of the government of the country, and are placed under very great and galling disabilities from which the other members of the British Empire are exempt, and which have reduced them to a state of utter helplessness. The existence, moreover, of the system of indentured emigration gives to the British Colonies and the outside world the impression that Indians as a whole, are no better than indentured coolies, who are looked upon as very little, if at all, above the slave. The present state of things makes the Indians feel that, though theoretically they are equal subjects of the King, they hold a very inferior position in the British Empire. Other Asiatic races also hold the same, if not a worse, view about India and her status in the Empire. Humiliating as this position of inferiority is to the Indian mind it is almost unbearable to the youth of India whose outlook is broadened by education and travel in foreign parts where they come in contact with other free races.

In the face of these grievances and disabilities, what has sustained the people is the hope and faith inspired by promises and assurances of fair and equal treatment which have been held out from time to time by our Sovereigns and British statesmen of high standing. In the crisis we are now going through, the Indian people have sunk domestic differences between themselves and the Government and have faithfully and loyally stood by the Empire. The Indian soldiers were eager to go to the battlefields of Europe, not as mercenary troops, but as free citizens of the British Empire which required their services, and her civilian population was animated by one desire, namely, to stand by England in the hour of her need. Peace and tranquillity reigned throughout India when she was practically denuded of British and Indian troops. The Prime Minister of England, while voicing the sentiments of the English people in regard to India's part in this great war, spoke of Indians as "the joint and equal custodians of one common interest and future."

What is Wanted

India does not claim any reward for her loyalty, but she has a right to expect that the want of confidence on the part of Government, to which she not unnaturally ascribes her present state, should now be a thing of the past and that she should no longer occupy a position of subordination but one of comradeship. This would assure the Indian people that England is ready and willing to help them to attain self-government under the ægis of the British Crown, and thus discharge the noble mission which she has undertaken and to which she has so often given voluntary expression through her rulers and statesmen. What is wanted is not merely good government or efficient administration, but government that is acceptaple to the people, because it is responsible to them. This is what, India understands, would constitute the changed angle of vision.

If after the termination of the war, the position of India practicslly remains what it was before and there is no materials change in it, it will undoubtedly cause bitter disappointment and great discontent in the country, and the beneficent effects of participation in common danger, overcome by common effort, will soon disappear, leaving no record behind save the painful memory of unrealised expectations. We feel sure that the Government is also alive to the situation and is contemplating measures of reform in the administration of the country. We feel that we should avail ourselves of this opportunity to respectfully offer to Government our humble suggestions as to the lines on which these reforms should proceed. They must, in our opinion, go to the root of the matter. They must give to the people real and effective participation in the government of the country, and also remove those irritating disabilities as regards the possession of arms and a military career, which indicate want of confidence in the people and place them in a position of inferiority and helplessness. With this view, we would take the liberty to suggest the following measures for consideration and adoption:—

Thirteen Recommendations

1 In all the Executive Councils, Provincial and Imperial half the number of members should be Indians; the European element in the Executive Councils should, as far as possible, be nominated from the ranks of men trained and educated in the public life of England, so that India may have the benefit of a wider outlook and larger experience of the outside world. It is not absolutely essential that the members of the Executive Councils, Indians or Europeans, should have experience of actual administration, for, as in the case of ministers in England, the assistance of the permanent officials of the departments is always available to them.

As regards Indians, we venture to say that a sufficient number of qualified Indians, who can worthily fill the office of members of the Executive Council and hold portfolios, is always available. Our short oxperience in this direction has shown how Indians like Sir S.P. Sinha, Sir Syed Ali Imam, the late Mr. Krishnaswami Iyer, Sir Shams-ul-Huda and Sir Sankaran Nair have maintained a high level of administrative ability in the discharge of their duties. Moreover, it is well known that the Native States, where Indians have opportunities, have produced renowned administrators like Sir Salar Jang, Sir T. Madhava Rao, Sir Sheshadri Aiyar, Dewan Bahadur Raghunath Rao, not to mention the present administrators in the various Native States of India.

The statutory obligation, now existing, that three of the members of the Supreme Executive Council shall be selected from the public services in India and similar provisions with regard to Provincial Councils should be removed. The etected representatives of the people should have a voice in the selection of the Indian members of the Executive Councils, and for that purpose a principle of election should be adopted.

2 All the Legislative Councils in India should have a substantial majority of elected representatives. These representatives, we feel sure, will watch and safeguard the interests of the masses and the agricultural population with whom they are in closer touch than any European officer, however sympathetic, can possibly be. The proceedings of the various Legislative Councils and the Indian National Congress and the Moslem League bear

ample testimony to the solicitude of the educated Indians for the welfare of the masses and their acquaintance with their wants and wishes.

The franchise should be broadened and extended directly to the people, Mahomedans or Hindus, wherever they are in a minority, being given proper and adequate representation having regard to their numerical strength and position.

3 The total number of the members of the Supreme Council should be not less than 150, and of the Provincial Councils not less than 100 for the major, and not less than 60 to 75 for the minor provinces.

4 The Budget should be passed in the shape of money bills, fiscal automony being conceded to India.

5 The Imperial Legislative Council should have power to legislate on, and discuss and pass resolutions relating to, all matters of Indian administration, and the Provincial Councils should have similar powers with regard to Provincial administrations save and except that the direction of military affairs, of foreign relations, declarations of war, the making of peace and the entering into treaties, other than commercial, should be vested in the Government of India. As a safeguard, the Governor-General-in-Council or the Governor-in-Council, as the case may be, should have the right of veto which, however, should be exercised subject to conditions and limitations.

The Position of the *Secretary of State*

6 The Council of the Secretary of State should be abolished The Secretary of State should, as far as possible, hold in relation to the Government of India a position similar to that which the Secretary of State for the Colonies holds in relation to the Colonies. The Secretary of State should be assisted by two permanent Under Secretaries, one of whom should be an Indian. The salaries of the Secretary and the Under Secretaries should be placed on the British estimates.

7 In any scheme of Imperial Federation, India should be given through her chosen representatives a place similar to that of the self-governing Dominions.

8 The Provincial Governments should be made autonomous, as stated in the Government of India's despatch, dated 29th August, 1911.

9 The United Provinces, as well as the other major provinces, should have a Governor brought from the United Kingdom and should have an Executive Council.

10 A full measure of local self-government should be immediately granted.

11 The right to carry arms should be granted to Indians on the same conditions as to Europeans.

12 Indians should be allowed to enlist as volunteers and units of a territorial army established in India.

13 Commissions in the army should be given to Indian youths under conditions similar to those applicable to Europeans.

The Signatories

The memorandum is signed by the following nineteen elected members:—Maharaja Sir Manindra Chandra Nandy, K. C. I. E., of Kasimbazar (Bengal Landholders), Mr. D. E. Wacha (Bombay), Mr. Bhupendranath Basu (Bengal), Rai Bahadur Bishan Dutt Shukul (Central Provinces Landholders), Pandit Madan Mohan Malaviya (United Provinces), Mr. K. V. Rangaswamiengar (Madras Landholders), Mr. Mazhar-ul Haque (Mahomedans of Behar and Orissa), Mr. V. S. Srinivasa Sastri (Madras), Dr. Tej Bahadur Sapru (United Provinces), Sir Ibrahim Rahimtoola, C. I. E. (Bombay), Rao Bahadur B. Narasimheswara Sarma (Madras), Khan Bahadur Mir Asad Ali Khan (Mahomedans of Madras), Mr. Kamini Kumar Chandra (Assam), Rai Bahadur Krishna Sahai (Behar and Orissa), Raja Rajendra Narayan Bhanja Deo of Kanika (Orissa Landholders), Mr. M. B. Dadabhoy, C. I. E. (Central Provinces), Rai Sita Nath Roy Bahadur (Bengal), Raja Sir Mahomed Ali Khan, K. C. I. E., of Mahmudabad (Mahomedans of the United Provinces), and Mr. Mahomed Ali Jinnah (Mahomedans of Bombay).

APPENDIX II

ENGLISH STATESMEN ON INDIA'S SERVICES

INDIA'S PRINCELY SUPPORT

Statement by Under Secretary of State

In reply to a question, Mr. CHARLES ROBERTS, Under Secretary of State for India, made the following statement in the House of Commons regarding the offers of help made in India in connexion with the war :—The Secretary of State for India has received the following telegram from the Viceroy, dated September 8, 1914 :

"Following is a summary of offers of service, money, etc., made in India to the Viceroy. The Rulers of the Native States in India, who number nearly seven hundred in all, have with one accord rallied to the defence of the Empire and offered their personal services and the resources of their States for the war. (Cheers.) From among the many Princes and Nobles who have volunteered for active service, the Viceroy has selected the Chiefs of Jodhpur, Bikaner, Kishangarh, Rutlam, Sachin, Patiala, Sir Pertab Singh, Regent of Jodhpur, the Heir-Apparent of Bhopal, and a brother of the Maharaja of Cooch Behar, together with other cadets of noble families. The veteran Sir Pertab would not be denied his right to serve the King-Emperor in spite of his seventy years, and his nephew, the Maharaja of Jodhpur, who is but sixteen years old, goes with him. (Cheers.)

"All these have, with the Commander-in-Chief's approval, already joined the Expeditionary Forces. The Maharaja of Gwalior and the Chiefs of Jaora and Dholpur, together with the Heir-Apparent of Palanpur, were, to their great regret, prevented from leaving their States. Twenty-seven of the larger States in India maintain Imperial Service Troops, and the services of every corps were immediately placed at the disposal of the Government of India on the outbreak of war. The Viceroy has accepted from twelve States contingents of cavalry, infantry, sappers, and transport, besides a camel corps from Bikaner, and most of them have already embarked.

"As particular instances of generosity and eager loyalty of the Chiefs, the following may be quoted :—Various Durbars have combined together to provide a hospitalship to be called 'The Loyalty' for the use of the Expenditionary Forces. The Maharaja of Mysore has placed Rs. 50 lakhs at the disposal of the Government of India for expenditure in connexion with the Expeditionary Force. The Chief of Gwalior, in addition to sharing in the expenses of the hospital ship, the idea of which originated with himself, and the Begum of Bhopal has offered to place large sums of money at the disposal of the Government of India and to provide thousands of horses as remounts. (Loud cheers.) From Loharu in the Punjab and Las Bela and Kalat in Baluchistan come offers of camels with drivers, to be supplied and maintained by the Chiefs and Sardars. Several chiefs have offered to raise additional troops for military service should they be required, and donations to the Indian Relief Fund have poured in from all States. The Maharaja of Rewa has offered his treasury, and even his private jewellery for the service of the King-Emperor. (Cheers.) In addition to contributions to the Indian Fund, some Chiefs—namely, those of Kashmir, Bundi, Orchha, and Gwalior and Indore—have also given large sums to the Prince of Wales' Fund. Maharaja of Kashmir, not content with subscribing himself to the Indian Fund, presided at a meeting of 20,000 people held recently at Srinagar and delivered a stirring speech, in response to which large subscriptions were collected.

"Maharaja Holkar offers, free of charge, all horses in his State Army which may be suitable for Government purposes. Horses also offered by Nizam's Government, by Jamnagar, and other Bombay States. Every Chief in the Bombay Presidency has placed the resources of his State at the disposal of Government, and all have made contributions to the Relief Fund. Loyal messages and offers have also been received from the Mehtar of Chitral and tribes of the Khyber Agency as well as the Khyber Rifles. Letters have been received from the most remote States in India, all marked by deep sincerity of desire to render some assistance, however humble, to the British Government in its hour of need.

"Last, but not least, from beyond the borders of India have been received generous offers of assistance from the Nepal

Durbar; the military resources of the State have been placed at the disposal of the British Government, and the Prime Minister has offered a sum of three lakhs of rupees to the Viceroy for the purchase of machine-guns or field equipment for British Gurkha Regiments proceeding overseas, in addition to large donations from his private purse to the Prince of Wales' Fund and the Imperial Indian Relief Fund. To the 4th Gurkha Rifles, of which the Prime Minister is honorary Colonel, the Prime Minister has offered Rs. 30,000 for the purchase of machine guns in the event of their going on service. The Dalai Lama of Tibet has offered 1,000 Tibetan troops for service under the British Government. His Holiness also states that Lamas, innumerable throughout the length and breadth of Tibet, are offering prayers for success of British Army and for happiness of souls of all victims of war.

"The same spirit has prevailed throughout British India. Hundreds of telegrams and letters have been received by Viceroy expressing loyalty and desire to serve Government either in the field or by co-operation in India. Many hundreds have also been received by local administrations. They come from communities and associations, religious, political, and social, of all classes and creeds, also from individuals offering their resources or asking for opportunity to prove loyalty by personal services. The following may be mentioned as typical examples :—The All-India Moslem League, the Bengal Presidency Moslem League, the Moslem Association of Rangoon, the Trustees of the Aligarh College, the Behar Provincial Moslem League, the Central National Mahomedan Association of Calcutta, the Khoja Community and other followers of Aga Khan, the Punjab Moslem League, the Mahomedans of Eastern Bengal, the citizens of Calcutta, Madras, Rangoon, and many other cities, the Behar Landholders' Association, the Madras Provincial Congress Committee, the Taluqdars of Oudh, the Punjab Chiefs' Association, the United Provinces Provincial Congress Committee, the Hindus of the Punjab, the Khalsa Diwan representing orthodox Sikhs, the Bohra Community, and the Parsee Community of Bombay.

"The Delhi Medical Association offer the field hospital that was sent to Turkey during Balkan War. Bengalee students offer enthusiastic services for an ambulance corps, and there were many other offers of medical aid. The Zemindars of Madras have offered 500 horses, and among other practical steps taken to assist Government may be noted the holding of meetings to allay panic, keep down prices, and maintain public confidence and credit. Generous contributions have poured in from all quarters to Imperial Indian Relief Fund." (Loud and prolonged cheers.)

STATEMENT BY THE SECRETARY OF STATE

The MARQUESS of CREWE made a statement to the House of Lords on September 9,1914, in substance similar to that made in the House of Commons by the Under Secretary for India, of what he called the wonderful series of offers of their resources in the cause of the Empire made by the Feudatory Princes and Ruling Chiefs of India, and read the King-Emperor's Message in response thereto. After giving the detailed account of the offers of service, money, and other help made to the Viceroy by the native Princes, Chiefs, and Rulers, and representative bodies of the Indian people, he said that similar offers had reached the Secretary of State from chiefs who happened to be at present in Europe. The Gaekwar of Baroda and Maharaja of Bharatpur, to mention two only, had placed the whole resources of their States at the disposal of his Majesty's Government. The Indian community in England, including the Indian students, had made loyal offers of services. He felt confident that the House and the country would feel deep appreciation of this magnificent demonstration of the loyalty with which the Princes and peoples of India had indentified themselves with the cause of the Empire. (Cheers.) He also said that he had received a telegram from the Viceroy describing what happened yesterday in the Legislative Council. The Viceroy, in opening the proceedings, read the message from the King Emperor, and then made a speech in which he said he was sure he was expressing the views of the whole of India in assuring his Majesty of unflinching loyalty and devotion. A resolution was moved declaring that the members of the Legislative Council, voicing the feelings which animated the whole of the people of India, desired to give expression to their feeling of unswerving loyalty and enthusiastic devotion to the King Emperor, and their unflinching support of the British Government. The resolution also stated the desire of the people of India, in addition to the military assistance afforded, to share in the heavy financial burdens imposed by the war. The resolution was supported by representatives of various races and creeds, and was carried without a single dissentient. Their lordships would agree that this demonstration of loyalty was one of the most gratifying facts as the outcome of the war—that the representatives of the various races of India should in so whole-hearted a manner rally round the British Government. He was sure their lordships would desire to express their appreciation of the part that India was playing in the great rally of the Empire. (Cheers.)

Speech by Lord Lansdowne

The MARQUESS of LANSDOWNE: The announcement by the noble marquess is one of surpassing interest, and one which will prove to be of historic importance in the annals of the British Empire. Let me, before I go further, express the admiration with which we listened to the words in which his Majesty was pleased to acknowledge the offer which the Goverment received from the people and Princes of India. It is indeed a wonderful series of offers. One and all of the peoples of India have come forward at this critical moment to assure us of their support in whatever form they are able to provide it. It is indeed a a great thing that those multitudinous races and peoples should have joined in this movement without reference to geographical divisions, religious differences, political divisions, or distinctions of race. We know how deep those cleavages are, and how often they separate one part of India from another. But in this case they were not allowed to prevail, and I am sure that the result will produce an immence impression not only on the people of this couutry, but on all who, no matter in what part of the world, are anxious spectators of the great struggle which is now proceeding. (Cheers.) I listened with special interest to that part of the noble marquess's speech in which he gave us an account of the manner in which the ruling Chiefs of India have come forward. There was a time when I had the honour of enjoying the friendship aud intimacy of a number of those Chiefs; and I left India with a profound impression of the sincerity of their desire to bear, whenever an opportunity was offered to them, a useful and honourable part in the affairs of the Empire. (Cheers.) Their generosity is proverbial. The word generosity is often accompanied by the word "princely," and in India we have every reason to be aware of what "princely generosity" means. But in this ease they have given us a great deal more. I well remember the pride which the great chiefs and rulers took in the Imperial Service Corps instituted in the time of my predecessor, Lord Dufferin. I know it was their ambition that those Imperial Service troops should not be merely extremely smart on parade, but should be given a chance of fighting alongside of our troops in the cause of the Empire. I heard with great interest the noble marquess's catalogue of the Princes who are to accompany the Indian force on this campaign, and I may perhaps be permitted to echo what he said with regard to one whom I am able to describe as an old personal friend of my own. I mean the Regent of Jodhpur, better known to his intimates as Sir Pertab Singh. I also heard with great satisfaction the noble marquess's account of the support which he was receiving from the Maharajah of Nepal. We owe a great debt to the Nepal Government (cheers), for it is with their assistance and concurrence we are able to raise those magnificent Gurkha regiments, of whom I am glad to know a certain number will accompany the Indian expedition.

The MARQUESS of CREWE: Seven battalions of Gurkhas. (Cheers.)

THE MARQUESS of LANSDOWNE: I doubt whether every one in this country realises how great a thing it is that those ruling chiefs should come forward in this way upon our side. I wonder, for example, whether every one realises that the Maharajah of Mysore, whose munificent gift the noble marquess referred to, rules over a population which exceeds the whole population of Sweden. I wonder whether any one calls to mind that the Maharajah of Gwalior, the Maharajah Scindia, has more subjects than the King of Denmark, or that the Nizam of Hyderabad governs a people twice as numerous as the people of the Netherland and three times as numeous as the people of Ireland. It is no small thing that those rulers, standing where they do in our Indian system, should have come forward without exception and given such practical proof of their desire to help us. I venture on the part of those who sit on this side of the House to congratulate the noble marquess on the manner in which the India Office has been supported at this critical time, and I add to that our congratulations to the Viceroy, to whom at a moment when he must have many sad preoccupations, the great response of India must bring consolation and encouragement. I am sure it will be the desire of the House that our cordial thanks should be conveyed to the people of India and the Indian chiefs who have stood by us in so conspicuous a manner. (Cheers.)

THE COST OF THE INDIAN EXPEDITIONARY FORCE

Lord Crewe

The Marquess of CREWE moved in the House of Lords on September 16, 1914 : "That, his Majesty having directed a military force consisting of British and Indian troops, charged upon the revenues of India, to be despatched to Europe or service in the war in which this country is engaged, this House consents that the ordinary pay and other ordinary charges of any troops so despatched, as well as the ordinary charges of any vessels belonging to the Government of India that may be employed in this expedition which would have been charged upon the resources of India if such troops or vessels had remained in that country or seas adjacent, shall continue to be so chargeable, provided that, if it shall be necessary to replace the troops or vessels so withdrawn by other vessels or forces, then the expenses of raising, maintaining, and providing such vessels and forces shall be repaid out of any moneys which may be provided by Parliament for the purpose of the said expedition." The enthusiasm which the sending of the Indian Expeditionary Force had evoked in India was (he said) a magnificent tribute to the justice of British rule there, and was evidence also of how high the heart of India beat in sympathy with the United Kingdom in this mighty conflict. It was the desire of India also that she ought not to profit in the sense of making any saving in consequence of the absence of her troops abroad. The precedents varied. In some cases India had been asked to defray the extra charges involved in the sending of her troops to other parts of the world; in other cases the entire cost had been undertaken by this country. The particular course taken in the motion was thought by India to be a perfectly fair one; and speaking without prejudice as to what might happen in the future, both as to the duration of the war and a number of other factors about which it was impossible to express any opinion, he submitted it to the House as an arrangement that was reasonable both from the Indian and British points of view.

Lord Curzon

Earl CURZON of KEDLESTON desired to take the opportunity of joining in the tribute of admiration of the splendid spirit of loyalty shown by all creeds and classes in India, and of congratulation to the Viceroy and the Government of India for the substantial and magnificent assistance which they had been able to give to the Empire in this crisis. In ordinary circumstances he might have felt some doubt in regard to the justice of the proposal submitted by the noble marquess. There had been fluctuations in our policy in the past, fluctuations, in some cases, not altogether creditable to our standard of chivalry and honour. Broadly speaking, the principle which was now observed was that when Indian troops were employed outside India the expenditure should not fall upon her revenue. That was so in the case of the expedition which he, as Viceroy of India in 1900, had the honour of sending for the relief of the Legations at Peking. But this particular case was exceptional. The troops of India were spontaneously taking part in a war which might be held to involve the interests of India as included in the whole Empire.

The Pay of British officers with the Force

Viscount MIDLETON referred to a letter which appeared in the "Times" of that day in regard to the payment of Indian officers on service in Europe, and said that probably the noble marquess would feel that there was very considerable hardship if officers, especially married officers, who had establishments in India on a certain rate of pay, were to suffer loss through giving up work in India and becoming equipped for foreign service. Whether the loss fell on the revenues of India or of this country, these officers should not be at any loss on account of going to serve his Majesty on the Continent. He hoped the noble marquess would give the subject his favourable consideration.

The Marquess of CREWE said his attention had been called to the letter in the "Times." The question was simple enough in the case of officers of the Indian Army, but probably the letter in the "Times" was written in the interest not of an officer in the Indian service, but of one of a British regiment that happened to be in India at the time, receiving there the increased rate of Indian pay, and now brought home to Europe; and in that case the question was not so simple. It might be felt by officers in some other British battalions serving almost alongside this one that it was hardly reasonable that officers in the same service should receive the far higher rate of pay, perhaps for a considerable period, than they themselves were receiving. There was also the further difficulty that a large number of officers, both in the Indian service and the Indian British regiments who were home on leave, had been detained and had gone to join the forces. On the whole, however, he was disposed to regard this claim with a great deal of sympathy. In a number of cases the establishment of wives and families had to be kept running in India for an indefinite period, and the sacrifice of the extra Indian pay might be a very serious matter. He was not able to make a definite promise, but he could assure the House that it was being carefully considered by his office as to how the claim could best be met.

The resolution was agreed to.

INDIA'S WILLING BURDEN

Mr. Asquith

Mr. ASQUITH, who was received with prolonged cheers, moved a resolution on the same day in the House of Commons in similar terms to the one adopted in the House of Lords with respect to the charges on the revenues of India of British and Indian troops employed in Europe. He said he was quite certain that the motion would be received with complete assent and gratitude in every quarter of this House. He did not think that in all the moving exhibitions of national and Imperial patriotism which the war had evoked there was any which had more touched, and rightly touched, the feelings of this House and the country than the message sent by the Viceroy of India announcing the magnificent response which the Princes and people of that country had made to our need. (Cheers.) In consequence of the provisions of Section 55 of the Government of India Act, 1858, it was not constitutionally right or proper to charge on the revenues of India except in the case of actual invasion or sudden and unforeseen emergency the cost of armed forces which might be sent outside that country. The assent of both Houses of Parliament was needed before any such charge could be imposed on the revenues of India. The assistance of the Indian Army in imperial exigencies had been more than once, indeed several times, since the passing of that Act, offered by India and accepted by ourselves. He would not go into the precedents, because it was not necessary to do so, but in most of those cases the whole cost of the charge had been met, as he was sure we would willingly meet it in this case, out of the revenues of the United Kingdom. But when this matter came up two or three weeks ago before the Legislative Council of the Viceroy of India, one of the unofficial Indian members moved a resolution to the effect that India would desire in the present emergency that she should be allowed not only to send her troops, but to contribute the cost of their maintenance and pay, and the Viceroy on behalf of the Government of India, and he was sure with the assent and sympathy not only of this House and the people of this country, but of the whole people of the British Empire, accepted that offer. The result was that through this patriotic initative not in any sense dictated or inspired by the Government, but proceeding from an unofficial member of the Council of India, these splendid British and Indian troops that were already upon their way, and which we believed would afford to us and to the Empire at large most effective assistance—(cheers)—in the righteous struggle in which we were engaged—(cheers)—these Indian troops would be sent, as far as their ordinary charges were concerned, at the expense of the Government and people of India. The resolution he had to move was of a purely formal character, and was necessary in order to comply with the requirements of the Act of Parliament. But he was sure the House would not be giving expression to what every one felt if it did not couple with its acceptance an assurance of its sincere and heartfelt appreciation of the spontaneous and splendid assistance which our great Dependency of India was giving us. (Loud cheers.)

Mr. Bonar Law

Mr. BONAR LAW said he was glad to have the privilege of seconding the resolution which had been moved. Since the war broke out nothing, as the Prime Minister had said, not even the heroic conduct of our own soldiers on the field of battle, had moved the people of this country more deeply than the spontaneous, the enthusiastic outburst of loyalty to their Emperor and patriotism to the Empire of which we had an account in the message of the Viceroy given the other day. (Cheers.) The circumstances under which this resolution was necessary were another proof of the reality and of the value of that assistance. Previously, when Indian troops, as the Prime Minister had pointed out, had been used out of India the Government of India had looked with a jealous eye in order to see that no part of the financial burden should fall on the people of India. Now, the Indian Government, representing and inspired by the Indian people, were not only sending their sons to risk their lives at the side of our own soldiers, by whom they would be proudly welcomed as comrades, but were insisting on bearing a share of the burden of the expense which was involved. He ventured to say the other day at the Guildhall that the moral forces which our enemies not only despised but affronted would prove in the long run stronger than the material forces on which only they relied. It was on moral forces that we relied to-day. The generous aid which was coming to us from the self-governing Dominions in every part of the Empire was coming of their own free will—it could not be demanded by us, and it could not be enforced by us. This assistance from India also was coming, not from force but from good will, and he believed that it was coming because, on the whole, every one who left this country to take part in the Government of India, from the Viceroy to the humblest official, was inspired by the tradition that it was his duty, not to exploit India for the benefit of this country, but to rule it for the good of the people of India. On the whole, we had succeeded, and it was because in the main the people of India recognized that that was the spirit in which the government was carried out that we had received so generously their assistance in our hour of need. (Cheers.)

THE INDIAN EXPEDITIONARY FORCE

Lord Kitchener

Earl KITCHENER, in the course of a statement on the campaign in the House of Lords on November 26, 1914, said that the arrival of the Indian divisions on the scene was of great assistance to Sir John French, and with French reinforcements which were being pushed up to the front, the Germans gradually realised that their public boasts to advance to Calais resembled closely their statement with regard to Paris. (Cheers.) Referring to the entrance of Turkey into the field against the Allics, he said:— At the end of October, without any warning, Turkey violated her neutrality by suddenly bombarding Odessa and other Black Sea ports. Previous to this she had already massed troops in order to invade Egypt, and armed Bedouins had crossed our frontier. We are now in touch with the advanced parties of the Turkish forces about 30 miles east of the Suez Canal. The hostile action of Turkey has further induced us to send an Indian expedition against the Turkish provinces at the northern end of the Persian Gulf. This force was twice met and twice defeated the Turkish troops, and has occupied the important town of Basra. (Cheers.) Active operations are also going on in South and East Africa.

Earl CURZON OF KEDLESTON thanked the Secretary of State for War for his reference to the Indian troops. It was indeed a source of delight to know that they had comported themselves on the field of battle with a gallantry not less than that of our European Allies or of the British comrades by whose side they were placed. He would like to join in the congratulations to the Indian troops for their singularly successful capture of the port of Basra. Anybody who knew the East knew that that exploit would ring throughout Asia, and would be regarded there not merely as the capture of a substantial position, but as a damaging blow to Turkish prestige.

INDIA'S WAR CONTRIBUTION

The Marquess of CREWE moved :—" That his Majesty, having directed military forces charged upon the revenues of India to be despatched out of India for service in the war in which this country is engaged, this House, in compliance with Section 55 of the Government of India Act, 1858, consents that the ordinary pay and other ordinary charges of any troops so despatched, or that may be so despatched during the continuance of the war, as well as the ordinary charges of any vessels belonging to the Government of India that may be employed in these expeditions which would have been charged upon the resources of India if such troops or vessels had remained in that country or seas adjacent, shall continue to be so chargeable provided that, if it shall be necessary to replace the troops or vessels so withdrawn by other vessels or forces, then the expense of raising, maintaining, and providing such vessels and forces shall be repaid out of any moneys which may be provided by Parliament for the purpose of the said expeditions." The motion, he said, was necessary under the Act of 1858. This was not the moment to attempt a nice calculation as to the direct interest of India. For the present all that need be done was to express their thanks to India for the generous and spontaneous manner in which she had come forward at this period to share the expense. (Cheers.)

Earl CURZON of KEDLESTON, on behalf of the Opposition, supported the motion, and it was agreed to.

THE INDIAN ARMY AND ITS SERVICE

Statement by the Under Secretary

Mr. CHARLES ROBERTS moved a resolution in the House of Commons on November 26, 1914, similar in terms to that moved in the House of Lords by the Marquess of Crewe, giving the sanction of the House to the ordinary expenses of the Indian Expeditionary Force operating in non-European countries being chargeable on the revenues of India. Two months ago, he said, the Prime Minister had moved in that House a motion relating to the despatch of the Indian forces to Europe: and under it the House of Commons gave its assent to the payment from Indian revenues of the ordinary charges of a force of British and Indian troops to be despatched to Europe for service during the present War. That resolution, however, did not sanction the application of Indian revenues to defray the cost of military operations outside India in non-European areas of the War, and it was, therefore, necessary to pass the present Supplementary Resolution, which gave a general assent to the contribution which India wished to make to the expenses of the Indian forces employed in any of the theatres of War, wherever they might be. It was not an oversight that the original Resolution did not cover the whole ground. Parliament had rightly surrounded with constitutional safeguards the application of Indian revenues to pay the cost of Indian expeditions outside the confines of India except in cases of invasion or unforeseen sudden emergency, and, therefore, it had been thought necessary to get the assent of both Houses of Parliament to meet the gap which it was now proposed to cover. India did not seek to make any saving out of the absence of the troops she would have had to pay for if they had remained in Indian cantonments. Therefore, it had been agreed, with the unanimous assent of the Legislative Council, that Indian revenues should continue to bear the normal expenses which they would have had to bear if the War had not taken place, while this country bore the extraordinary expenses involved in the despatch of troops to the theatre of War. That was the financial arrangement under the previous Resolution. It was proposed to follow that precedent in the present Supplementary Resolution, but it must be understood that it was not a hard and fast rule, and was liable to subsequent modification by agreement, and with the assent of Parliament, according to the nature of the operations in which the Indian troops might be engaged. In any case, we had warmly to recognise the substantial help which was being afforded to the Empire by the appearance of Indian troops at a great number of points in a battl-line which extended from Tsingtau to La Bassee across the breadth of three Continents. (Cheers.)

So much for the purely technical and formal aspect of this Motion. But he had been asked a little while ago to explain the absence of the customary Budget statement in reference to Indian finances, and he desired to take that opportunity of making it plain that the postponement was not due to any inattention or indifference to Indian questions. Indeed, there never was a time when the interest in Indian questions and the feeling of good-will between England and India was more widespread or more strong than at present. (Cheers). All the documents required by Statute had been presented to Members of the House of Commons but, just as our own domestic discussions had had to be postponed, so the discussion on some Indian points had better be taken at a later date. But he did not think they would suffer by the delay, and he hoped that circumstances might admit that, later on in the present Session, the customary Budget discussion on Indian affairs would take place.

The Censor and the Public

There had been some complaints in the papers, both here and in India, as to the meagre details which had been given of the work of the Indian troops. It was known, of course, that they had taken part in the reduction of Tsingtau, in the rapid and successful occupation of Fao and Basra in the Persian Gulf, that they are in force in Egypt, that they took part in the landing at Shaik Said, and that, sharing the vicissitudes of war, they were present at an attack against great odds in East Africa. Of course, the main force was in France, taking part in battles which were taking even longer to decide than the famous battle of the great Indian epic, which lasted eighteen days before it was concluded. All were agreed that it was exceptionally necessary in the case of India that full details of the work of the Indian troops should be given, and arrangements had been made towards that end. There were official reporters who were sending summaries of the doings of the Indian troops, which were telegraphed to India, and we were pleading with the Military Censor to give as much information as military necessities would allow. On the other hand, every one would recognise that ever since the debacle at Sedan, which was undoubtedly facilitated by the publication of news in the London newspapers, the military censorship in all countries was growing stricter and stricter. It was, of course, a strain on our natural anxieties, but every endeavour was being made to give as much news as possible. There was also one special disadvantage in reference to the Indian troops. The newspaper accounts had mainly referred to gallant behaviour on the part of the Sikhs and Gurkhas, and they fully deserved all the recognition which they had obtained. But there were other Indian races who were represented—Pathans, Jats, Dogras, Punjabi Mussulmans, Rajputs, Mahrattas and others—whose doings had been somewhat overlooked. Of the actual exploits of the troops the official reports, private letters and the accounts of eye-witnesses all told the same story. There was no need to speak of the quality of the British units in the Indian Army, or of the very gallant leadership of the officers with the Indian Troops, but the Indian troops themselves had, by all accounts, acquitted themselves in accordance with the expectations of those who best knew their courage and training. (Cheers.) They very soon adapted themselves to conditions of fighting which were as novel to them as to the British troops. They had stood the shell fire steadily, and when the time came to give the details of their action in the recent fighting it would be a record of which both India and England would be proud. (Cheers.) He hoped he might also be allowed to bear testimony to the energy of the Viceroy during the outbreak of this War. The varied expeditions which had been despatched from India showed the energy which he had displayed in the midst of personal griefs and anxieties, for the organization of the Lady Hardinge Hospital in this country was a reminder of a sorrow which is still recent, and the House knew that his son, on whom the D. S. O. had been conferred, had been severely wounded. (Hear, hear.) They had to express sincere sympathy and admiration for the energy with which the resources of India had been marshalled in the service of the Empire. Perhaps he might also be allowed to bear testimony to the invaluable services of the Commander-in-Chief, Sir Beauchamp Duff, and to express also the great sympathy of the House with him in the loss which he had sustained in the death of his son in the War. (Hear hear.)

The Loyalty of the Princes

He hoped the House would bear with him if he added a word or two about the loyalty which India had displayed during the despatch of these expeditions. It was always difficult, at a distance from any country, to be sure that one gauged and interpreted rightly the feeling of that country, but he thought one could distinguish certain different notes as one read the mass of telegrams, resolutions, manifestos, speeches and newspaper articles in which Indian opinion had expressed itself. It was quite impossible to summarise them, but one noted first the fighting spirit of many of the Ruling Chiefs who at once despatched telegrams pleading in urgent and insistent terms their personal claim to serve the King-Emperor upon the battlefield. (Cheers.) He would quote one picturesque phrase which struck him in one telegram. It ran as follows :—"The noise of battle is lulling music to Rajput blood." That was the spirit of the Maharajas who are at the front—the veteran Sir Pertab Singh and his young nephew, and the Maharajas of Bikanir and Kishengarh. Would the House allow him to quote another telegram which the Maharaja of Bikanir sent :—

"I and my troops are ready and prepared to go at once to any place, either in Europe or India, or wherever services might be usefully employed in the interest of safety honour, and welfare of our Sovereign and his Dominions. Your Excellency knows the traditions of the Rathor Bika Rajputs. We long to be early at the front, but whether my troops can be used at present or not, I would earnestly ask your Excellency at least to give me myself an opportunity for that personal military service of the King-Emperor and the Empire, which is my highest ambition as a Rathor Chief and as a member of His Imperial Majesty's Staff."

The Maharaja had had his wish. He was in France at the front, and his Camel Corps had been doing very useful service in the peninsula of Sinai. Might he add one other telegram? This was sent by the Nizam of Hyderabad, the Mahomedan ruler of the largest Indian State, who said :—

"At this crisis I beg that your Excellency will lay before His Majesty the King-Emperor the assurance that my heart beats at one with that of all the loyal people of Great Britain and her Dominions throughout the world and that my sword and the whole resources of my State are His Majesty's to command for England and the Empire."

It was very difficult to acknowledge adequately all the princely munificence of the ruling chiefs in connexion with the expedition. The generosity of the Maharaja of Jaipur and that of the Maharaja of Gwalior might be mentioned as instances. The Maharaja of Gwalior, besides princely contributions to every fund started in England or India, running into many thousands of pounds, had organised, jointly with the Begum of Bhopal, a hospital ship and had given a large contribution of horses. His latest munificent gift was a fully equipped motor ambulance fleet. Ill-health alone, to his grievous disappo ntment, had prevented him from taking the field in person.

A Tribute to the Educated Classes

A wave of instinctive and emotional loyalty had swept over the people of India. But it would be unfair not to recognise that besides this, there is among the Indian educated classes a loyalty based on reason and the recognition of facts. It was at times less warmly expressed, but was none the less substantial. It was sensible of the undeniable benefits conferred by British rule. It regarded—not to put the case too high—the present regime as the best working arrangement for India. It was satisfied that within the framework of the Empire legitimate hopes and aspirations could in due time be met. This more sober sentiment found expression also among those Moslem who could not but feel the strain on their religious sympathies imposed by the insensate folly of Turkey's attack upon the British Empire. Men like the Nizam of Hyderabad and the Aga Khan had been unhesitating in the advice they had given to those with whom their views would naturally carry weight. Indian Moslems had, he believed, made up their minds that their secular allegiance was due to the King-Emperor. They knew that their religion obtained the ampiest toleration and respect in the British Empire, and that the idea that the present War was a religious war was an absurdity. The matter was perhaps summed up in the remark of an Indian Mussulman :—" Why should anyone question the loyalty of India? Is it not our Empire, too?" (Cheers).

An Executive Council for the United Provinces

What was happening before our eyes did, at all events, vindicate the policy that had been adopted and was being worked out in India—the policy of enlisting the co-operation of Indians in the work of Government. There was no finality in the task of adjusting the machinery of government to Indian conditions and to the new forces that our own action had evoked. For the time being, as everyone recognised, administrative and constitutional problems were necessarily in abeyance, but he wished to take this opportunity of announcing a change in the Constitution of one of the provinces which was in course of settlement before the outbreak of the War. It was not a change of a very far-reaching character, and the Secretary of State and the Viceroy saw no reason in the existence of the War to postpone the announcement. The Secretary of State had asked him to state that he had approved the proposal of the Governor-General in Council to create a small Council in the United Provinces to assist the Lieutenant-Governor in the executive government of the province. (Cheers.) A draft of the necessary Proclamation would be laid in due course before Parliament. This would give to the United Provinces a machinery of government similar to that which obtains in the larger provinces of India. It would, incidentally, enable an Indian to serve as a member of the highest Executive Council in the province. He would add that the establishment of the council has the support of the Viceroy and of the Lieutenant-Governor. (Cheers.)

The Aftermath of the War

For the rest, it was premature to attempt to anticipate the consequences that might follow from this striking and historic event—the participation of India in force in the World-War of the Empire. (Cheers.) The results would not be fully seen until the War was over. But it was clear that India claimed to be not a mere dependant of, but a partner in, the Empire, and her partnership with us in spirit and on the battlefields could not but alter the angle from which we should all henceforward look at the problems of the government of India. (Cheers.) He thought he might call the attention of the House of Commons to one possible illustration of this change in the point of view. It must be a source of pride and satisfaction to India that she had sent the first of the great contingents from the Over-Seas Dominions into the European theatre of War, and that one of her brave soldiers, if the newspaper statements were correct, had been recommended for the coveted distinction of the Victoria Cross. (Cheers.) Indian Armies were soon to be followed by troops from Canada,

Australia, New Zealand, and South Africa. He need not allude to points of friction that had existed between India and some other parts of the Empire, though he was glad to remember that the difficulties in South Africa had been overcome. But he would refer to the summary of the Viceroy's speech in the Legislative Council during the debate on the despatch of the troops a few weeks ago. He said :—"There is nothing like comradeship in arms and joint participation in the dangers and hardships of war to level distinctions, inspire mutual respect, and foster friendship." He added :—"I cannot help feeling that as a consequence better relations will be promoted amongst the component parts of the British Empire. Many misunderstandings will be removed and outstanding grievances will be settled in an amicable and generous manner. In this sense, out of evil good may come to India, and this is the desire of us all." (Cheers.) That wish was shared also by the Secretary of State and would be echoed in the House of Commons. In the atmosphere of friendship and good-will which unite India and England to-day there was surely a bright hope for the future. (Cheers.) India must feel that East and West were engaged in a military partnership which, as we believed, was both for the benefit of the Indian peoples and for the Empire as a whole, and he could not but trust that the common endeavours of these days will enable India to realise that she was occupying, and was destined to occupy, a place in our free Empire worthy alike of her ancient civilization and thought, of the valour of her fighting races, and of the patriotism of her sons. (Cheers.)

THE RESPONSE OF INDIA

Mr. Charles Roberts, M. P., at Sheffield

Mr Charles Roberts, M. P., Under Secretary of State for India, visited Sheffield on February 25, 1915, and gave an address at the Victoria Hall on "The Response of India." Mr. H. A. FISHER, Vice-Chancellor of the University of Sheffield, presided, and was supported by the Lord Mayor (Councillor O. C. Wilson) and other leading citizens.

Mr. ROBERTS said that India's loyalty during the past six months had left an indelible impression upon Englishmen, and that generous outpouring of hers would not easily be forgotten. The Viceroy had told us that no fewer than 200,000 men had been, or were being, withdrawn from India for service in the various theatres of war. That was no small contribution of effective fighting force to our cause, and it was accompanied by a handsome money contribution.

There were two points, he thought, which had their influence on the attitude of the ruling chiefs. The pledged word that Britain gave to Belgium had also been given to guarantee their State : and they felt in a special sense their tie of personal allegiance to their Emperor. India's politicians had been as outspoken and unswerving in their support as the fighting races. At the Indian National Congress, held last December in Madras, there was a fine scene of patriotic enthusiasm when the resolution of loyal support was unanimcusly carried. He would like to add a word of recognition and thanks to those Indian students in England who formed themselves into an ambulance corps and accepted the rough and tumble of war in order to render service to their wounded fellow-countrymen.

The Claim to a Share in the Empire

The real innerness of this striking manifestation of loyalty was, he believed, to be found in the desire of the Indian peoples that Indian soldiers should take part in the war side by side with their British comrades. The great withdrawal of troops from India was proof of the general trust and confidence which could safely be reposed in the loyalty of the Indian people, and nothing that had occurred during the past seven months had in any degree betrayed that confidence. Had Britain, as in the Boer War, regarded the struggle as a sahibs' war, in which India took no part, that way danger lay ; for it would have denied India's share in the Empire of which she forms part.

He was constantly asked how had the Indian troops acquitted themselves. The answer was that they had acquitted themselves as those who knew them best expected of them. (Applause.) They had fought in a far-flung line of battle; and as to the spirit in which they had fought, two Indians, as was known, had, for the first time, won the coveted distinction of the V. C.

A Blow for the Pessimists

There were two further reflections he wished to make. The outburst of loyalty was no cause of surprise, although it was a source of gratification, to those who knew India best. But it must have been a real blow to the pessimists who in recent years had exaggerated what they called the spirit of Indian unrest. It was an elementary blunder to confuse a small criminal revolutionary group, whose crimes had sternly to be repressed, with the constitutional agitation that pursued the changes it advocated by an appeal to reason and justice, and loyally desired to work out those changes within the framework of the British Empire. The war had shown these things in their right perspective.

Indian Co-operation In Administration

Certainly it did nothing to dissuade Englishmen from their policy of associating Indians with the work of government. This wise policy had borne good fruit in the critical testing time. Every one must see that it had not reached its final stage. He would not suggest anything so absurd as to say that India, with its ancient civilisation and its deep attachment to immemorial customs, could be treated as though it was a brand—new Western State of the American Union. But he trusted to the good sense of Britons and Indians alike gradually to work out a system of government as an outgrowth of Indian traditions and adapted to Indian needs which would in due time meet the legitimate aspirations of India.

Secondly, he would ask them specially to recognise the admirable loyalty that had been shown by the Moslems of India. They plainly saw that this was not a religious war but a political war against the ambitions of Germany for world-domination. Our Government had given the pledge that the holy places of the Moslem faith should be immune from attack by ourselves, and had obtained the assent of our Allies to a similar promise, while ruling princes, like the Nizam of Hyderabad, and leaders of Mahomedan thought like the Aga Khan, had been unswerving in the sagacious advice which they had given to their co-religionists. Islam was not only a religion. It was a civilisation with a great past, a distinctive character, and a tradition that made its appeal to millions of men and whatever might be the political consequences to Turkey of its deplorable blunder, Islam would remain a world-force.

Reforms After The War

It was being asked in some quarters:-Why were not immediate steps being taken to meet Indian claims ? Why were not practical grievances being settled out of hand, such as those connected with the Arms Act, the Volunteers, or the question of commissions in the Indian Army ? He had no wish to put in a mere dilatory plea for delay. But the immediate task was to concentrate all endeavours for victory in the war. The minds of statesmen and administrators were too pre-occupied for controversial discussion. Measures, even if accepted in principle, often required prolonged consideration before the details could be properly adjusted. It was not fair to friendly critics, who might be entitled to a hearing, to stifle discussion by an appeal to patriotism, but an appearance of discord and disunion should encourage the enemy. In India the idea of a truce for the time being had been readily accepted. It was not really a question, as it was, of rewarding Indians for good behaviour. Indians themselves had repudiated the suggestion. Something much more fundamental was at stake, and that was the consolidation of right feeling between Britain and India. That right feeling should not come as a mere wave of passing emotion. It should crystalise into a permanent attitude of mind. If that could be won as the lasting outcome ,of the war, public opinion in this country would be ready to adjust itself to such modifications as might prove to be necessary in the government of India, and the solution of the practical problems would follow accordingly. There were obstacles enough in the way. Let not mere unregenerate colour prejudice and racial feeling be added to them. Such persons as were afflicted with that malady should, since the world was wide, turn to work that would bring them in contact with none but their own kith and kin. Once let Englishmen concede the reciprocal superiorities of different races and the free scope for outstanding ability, whatever the caste or colour or creed of its possessor might be, and he did not think Indians would need to quarrel with them.

Would they allow him in passing to suggest that it would be well if the Press and people generally would give up talking about "natives" or "natives of India"? These expressions were now felt in India to be discourteous, though he was sure they were often used merely to describe those whose birthplace was India, without any knowledge that the phrase was disliked.

Indians and the Empire

It was wide of the mark to suggest that Indians were not a grateful people, or that the benefits of the British connexion were not recognised by them.

There was, however, one point in the relations of India to the Empire which could not be regarded with satisfaction. Last year, under the British Nationality and Status of Aliens Act, we established for the first time a uniform citizenship for the whole British Empire. But those Empire-wide rights did not include the free admission to all parts of the Empire. The control of immigration was vested in the self-governing Dominions, and Canada and Australia practically made it impossible for Indians to enter their territories, which the Dominions wished to reserve as white man's country. Recently, there was serious friction between the South African Government and the Indian settlers in South Africa, though that particular difficulty had been happily arranged by a practically complete agreement. Let them hope that the settlement of one controversy might form a precedent of good augury in other cases. And here again the war might be trusted to pave the way to a better state of feeling, a greater spirit of generosity, a larger sense of the claims of the Empire as a whole.

The Hopes of the Future

In a speech delivered the other day in India, the complaint was made that the Anglo-Indian bureaucracy pointed out "no land of promise" to the people of India. Perhaps it was rather the tendency of administrators to get on with the job in hand. Yet from the very nature of the case he thought that the future of India offered full scope for the aspirations of its sons. It was, as it seemed to him, a land where a growing measure of self-government in accordance with the special conditions of India was being progressively worked out as the fitness for self-government was proved, and the whole great experiment was like nothing that had ever existed before in the world. Then, as if that were not enough, the war had opened out new vistas. India no longer was to live as she did in past ages, apart in her own world. Now, and in the future, her life would blend with the main current of the world-movement, opening out into the central stream of history; and her sons before our eyes would consciously claim their part in the common heritage of the great Empire which, as we believed, stood for freedom and international right, and which had been truly said to be the greatest secular agency for good, now existing in the world. Was the land of promise not visible there ? (Loud applause.)

On the motion of the Lord Mayor, seconded by Colonel H. Hughes, a hearty vote of thanks was passed to Mr. Roberts.

INDIA'S PARTICIPATION IN THE WAR

Viscount Bryce presided at a meeting of the Indian Section of the Royal Society of Arts on March, 18, 1915, when Lieut. Col. A. C. Yate gave a lecture on "The Indian Army."

Lord Bryce on Indian Devotion

Lord Bryce, in opening the discussion, said that the story of the Indian troops was inextricably bound up with the whole romantic history of British Rule in India. One of the most interesting things in Indian and British history was the ability which our people seemed to possess, perhaps beyond that of any European race, to get into touch with the natives of another country and another language, to secure their loyalty and attachment, to enter into their feelings, and show themselves apt leaders of brave men. Colonel Yate had suggested what a magnificient training ground the experience in India was for many great British soldiers. It was the experience of Wellesley in India that made him to be chosen at the darkest hour of England's fortunes to go out and take command of our troops in the Peninsula and begin that career of conquest which ended at Waterloo—the greatest contest in which Britain had been engaged up to the present war. During all those years there had been ripening in the Indian Army that spirit of loyalty and devotion to its leaders as there had been ripening among us that appreciation of the noble qualities of the Indian troops, both of which had now found the most remarkable expression in the events of the last eight months—by far the most remarkable events in the whole long and brilliant history of the Indian Army. It was impossible to conceive a more striking instance of the loyalty and attachment of the people and princes and troops of India to the British Empire than the spontaneous offer which touched us all in August last. Since then by deeds of brilliant valour, the Indian troops had shown themselves the worthy compeers of our own troops and the troops of our Allies in their courage, devotion and endurance of all hardships. It was one of the redeeming incidents of a time full of sorrow. It was a new tie, and perhaps the deepest and most binding of all the ties that hereafter would unite us to India, because it showed that the efforts which we had made to discharge worthily the duties which Providence had laid upon us in India had been appreciated in India, and it showed that the people of India recognised that the future had in store for them and for us a closer connection than ever before based upon this endurance of common suffering and upon this devotion to a common cause. We might reasonably hope that our relations to India would rest upon a surer foundation of mutual affection and respect than was possible before, and that there would now be a feeling of common interest and common pride in the glory of the Empire and of common devotion to its welfare.

VALOUR OF INDIAN TROOPS

Sir Francies Younghusband

In a paper read by Sir Francis Younghusband at a meeting of the Royal Colonial Institute on May 11, 1915, he paid a glowing tribute to the valour of the Indian army. The Indian soldier, said Sir Francis, came upon the scene at a crucial moment, and did a service for the Empire for which the Empire owed him gratitude. The seventy thousand troops from India arrived in France when the German, foiled in their rush on Paris, were making their tremendous lunge at Calais. Just at the moment when the British line thin to breaking point, had to hold back the incessant and terrific onslaught of the Germans, this contingent of troops from India came upon the scene, and in their first serious action, on October 28, carried the village Neuve Chapelle, since become so famous. Had we not been to bring these reinforcements from India, had our position there been so precarious that we could not afford to take them away, and *a fortiori* had we been under necessity to send out more British troops to strengthen our position in India, then in all probability our troops in Flanders would not have been able to stay the German onrush, and our brave little army would have been swept off the Continent. That Indians were able to help the French, the Belgians and ourselves in stopping a blow which the Germans had prepared for years is a thing of which they may be proud, and for which we should always be grateful to them.

A Reservoir of Strength

India (continues Sir Francis) instead of being a strain and drain on England, was found to be a reservoir of strength, sending out men to project the heart of Empire, to protest the line of communications between England and India, to guard the gates ways to India, to attack the enemy's possessions.

The credit of this is due, in the first place, to the warm-heartedness and instinctive loyalty of the Indian people and in the second place, to the right-mindedness with which the British have sought to fulfil their trust to India. Whatever other qualities the people of India have, they have certainly a great capacity for affection. They show an extraordinary degree of devotion to individual Englishmen and women, and unbounded affection for such a ruler as Queen Victoria. They are not a cold-blooded race. They have quick warm hearts and they have an innate sense of loyalty to their rulers. The credit of what India did last autumn must therefore in the first place go to them. ... ... We, who have completed our service in India and can look back over our careers can see the harm we may have done by many unwitting roughness and rudeness and much unconscious harshness and discourtesy, arising in our earlier days from sheer ignorance and lack of sympathy and imagination.

The Settlement after the War

Discussing the settlement after the war, Sir Francis Young husband said :

Such deep emotions have been loosened, so many interest aroused and hopes raised, so much new light has been shed and experience gained, that men returning from wars in Europe, in Egypt, in Turkey, in Mesopotamia, in East Africa and in China will be men with a wider outlook and larger demands than they ever had before. And the Indian public, educated by not only keenly watching but by actually participating in the mighty happenings of these times, will be a different people from what they were before the war commenced. All will take time to settle down, and when they do it will not be to things as they were before. It will be to a new order to which they will have to accommodate themselves. And in the process of adjusting themselves to these new conditions there must necessarily be trouble, friction, discontent. It will be no easy process; and problems of extraordinary delicacy and complexity are already looming on the horizon. The old demand of Indians for commissions in the Army will be pressed ; and it seems so reasonable and fair to grant it to men who have fought so loyally and well. But if the fighting in France has taught us one thing more forcibly than another, it is the need of still more British officers with Indian regiments. It is a thorny subject, beset with difficulties, and one which, whether it is left alone or settled, is certain to cause discontent in common quarter.

India and the Colonies

Another still more difficult question is the admission of Indians to the Colonies. That was delicate enough before the war. How much more delicate will it be after it ? When India has taken such a prominent part in the defence of the Empire, how discontented she would be if there remains any part of it from which her people were still refused admission ?

A more definite share in the Councils of the Empire ; a larger part in the management of their own affairs ; a higher status altogether ; the right to bear arms and to volunteer ; a more equal social position-all those demands will be pressed. And the Chiefs who have stood so nobly by us may well hope to be granted a more prominent and effective part in the affairs of the Empire.

In regard to these difficulties, the experience we have gained in the war will help us to a solution. The thought of German lust for domination and habit of domineering, the degree to which Germany became intoxicated with power and the blindness with which it was exercised, disposes us to search out our own hearts to see whether we also may not unconsciously have been guilty of a similar sin. And even if we acquit ourselves of guilt we may at least recognise what we may be led to if we are not carefully on our guard. For there is in power something peculiarly blinding and dulling to the moral sense, and only those of the quickest sensibility and swiftest imagination are fitted to exercise it over peoples weaker than themselves.

After the war we may expect that the Indians will make, with increasing insistence, the demands I have mentioned for a greater share in the management of their own affairs. But in dealing with this question, we may lay fast hold of this fact that the leaders of Indian opinion and the great mass and bulk of the people have not the slightest desire, hope of ambition to sever the tie with England. In making their demands it is not severance but autonomy at which they aim ; Self-Government, indeed, they want ; but Self-Governmet within the Empire, not outside it.

"COMRADESHIP AND CO-OPERATION"

India's answer to Germany

The Lord Mayor of London presided at a great meeting held at the Guildhall on May 19,1915, under the auspices of the Central Committee for National Patriotic Organizations for the purpose of giving public expression to the Empire's sense of gratitude for the efforts and sacrifices made in the prosecution of the war by the self-governing Dominions, the Colonies and Protectorates and India. The Prime Minister and Mr. Bonar Law were the principal speakers, and among those present were the Marquess of Crewe, Mr. Lewis Harcourt, the Official representatives in London of Canada, Australia, New Zealand, and South Africa, Major-General Maharaja Sir Pertab Singh, the Jam Sahib of Nawanagar, the Raja Sahib of Akalkot, Captain the Raja of Barwani, Lord Reay, Lord Islington, Lord George Hamiltons

Lord Harris, Mr. Edwin Montague, Mr. Ameer Ali, Sir Krishna Gupta, Sir Mancherjee Bhownagree, Sir Guy Fleetwood Wilson, Mirza Abbas Ali Baig, and Mr. A. Yusuf Ali.

The Prime Minister's Speech

Mr. ASQUITH moved the following resolution: "That this meeting of the citizens of London records, on behalf of the British people, its abiding gratitude for the unparalleled services rendered by the self-governing Dominions, the Colonies, the Protectorates, and the Indian Empire, in the struggle to maintain the ideal of Liberty and Justice, which is the common and sacred cause of the Allies." We were, he said, well on in the tenth month of the greatest war in which we or any other people had ever been engaged. At home we had every reason to bestir ourselves. Our shores were, geographically, at any rate, within striking distance of the enemy, and the main theatre of war was nearer to London than our own northern counties. It was not so with our fellow-subjects to whose magnificent comradeship and co-operation we were paying our tribute of gratitude that day. They were far removed from the sphere of conflict, and now that the high seas had been cleared of hostile cruisers, their seaborn commerce pursued almost its normal course. But they were sons and daughters of the Empire. What touched us, touched them.

What India has done

After passing in review the contributions to the common cause, both in money and in men, of the Dominions, and the gallant services rendered by the Colonial troops, Mr. ASQUITH proceeded :—

Let me say one word now about India. (Cheers.) A White Paper was presented to Parliament last September enumerating the gifts and offers of service from the Princes and peoples of India. (Cheers.) As is apparent to any one who studies that return they have come from all quarters, and upon the most prodigal scale ; but even so, they have since been largely supplemented and increased. I will just select two or three instances simply as samples from this long and splendid catalogue. The Maharaja of Mysore made an enormous money contribution—one of the finest and most munificent that has come from any part of the Empire. That great feudatory, the Nizām of Hyderabad, contributed £400 to the expenses of the Imperial Service Lancers and the 20th Deccan Horse. The Maharaja of Gwalior have contributed—the list is so long that I hardly like to read it—with an amount of care and prevision which is beyond all praise, to almost every department which needed help and support. And I am glad to put it on record that his Majesty the King has just accepted a most generous offer of machine-guns from the Maharaja of Nepaul—(cheers)—a gift which is the expression of his intense desire—and it is a desire which is not founded upon obligation, but upon goodwill and sympathy—to contribute to the actual resources of the British Government in war material.

Our fellow-subjects in India itself have not been behindhand. They have raised a very large Imperial Indian Relief Fund, and the three Presidencies—Bengal, Madras and Bombay—have each had separate funds of their own which have been devoted on a large scale, and with the best results, mainly to the relief and support of the troops whom India has sent out.

What shall I say about the Indian forces? (Cheers.) India has put in the field, in the several theatres of war, including British troops sent from India, a force equivalent to nine complete infantry divisons, with artillery—(cheers) and eight cavalry brigades—(renewed cheers)—as well as several smaller bodies of troops aggregating more than an infantry division, in minor and outlying spheres. Putting the same thing in another way, India has placed at the disposal of the Empire, for service out of India, twenty-eight regiments of cavalry, British, Indian, and Imperial Service, and no less than 124 regiments of infantry, British, Indian, and Imperial. (Loud cheers.)

Then, again, when we look to the actual achievements of the forces so spontaneously despatched, so liberally provided, so magnificently equipped, the battlefields of France and Flanders bear undying tribute to their bravery and devotion. (Cheers.) I repeat what I said a few minutes ago, that I make no apology for entering into these details. They teach in a concrete form, which is better than any rhetoric, the truth that the Empire is one in purpose and one at heart. (Cheers.)

Mr. Bonar Law

Mr. Bonar Law, in seconding the resolution, said that when a venomous reptile was let loose, there was only one thing to be done, that was to destroy it. But in order to accomplish that task we needed—and, thank Heaven, we had behind us—the full force not only of the United Kingdom, but of the British Empire. (Cheers.) Our enemies had singled us out from all the Allies as the chief object of their hatred. The British Empire was the antithesis of everything for which German militarism stood. They relied on force, and force alone. They not only despised but they did not understand, moral forces and it was moral forces on which the British Empire rested. (Cheers.)

The Prime Minister had spoken of what had been done for us, let us say, by our Indian fellow-subjects. We knew some thing of it: but he did not think we fully realised here how much those men who had fought and died by the side of our own soldiers had helped us through these long months. (Cheers.) It was his belief that as a nation we had more reason to be proud of the spontaneous enthusiasm on behalf of their Emperor and their Empire of the Indian Princes and peoples than we had to be proud of the conquest of India. (Cheers.)

He did not wish in anything to look beyond this war. (Cheers.) Our enemies said it was we who organised it. What could we gain by it? What can we gain by it now? Nothing except peace, and security for peace in the future. (Cheers.) But perhaps he might be permitted to say for himself, and himself alone, not attempting to speak for any party, that he had now a hope that we should gain something more as the result of this war. The Dominions of the British Empire had not been created by the war, but the conditions had been changed by the war, and it was his hope, and if it was taken up in earnest while the metal was still glowing red hot from the furnance of war, he believed it could be done, that as a result of it we might see a Parliament of the British Empire, in which every part of that Empire, in proportion to its resources and its numbers, would share in the duty and the honour of ruling the British Empire. (Loud cheers.)

The resolution was unanimously carried and acknowledged by Mr. C. H. PERLEY (Canada), Sir GEORGE REID (Australia), Mr. T. MACKENZIE (New Zealand), and Mr. SCHREINER (South Africa).

Lord Crewe

The MARQUESSE of CREWE, in moving a vote of thanks to the Lord Mayor, desired to express his conviction that the recognition by that meeting of the answer which India had given to Germany would thrill through the whole of the Empire. That answer had been given by the Indian Army, by the Princes of India, and by the whole people of India, who had lavished their labour, their gifts, and their prayers on behalf of the cause of which their beloved King-Emperor was the centre and the symbol. (Cheers.) Of the hopes of the future Mr. Bonar Law had spoken eloquently, and he, for his part, would like also to think that the association of India and the Colonies at such a gathering as that was a significant sign of the essential comprehension which, as the years rolled on, would, as he firmly believed, sweep away all those obstacles of distance, of creed, or of race, which seemed to interfere with the complete union of the different members of the great Imperial Confederation—a union which would hinge upon the free activities of each, and which would be firmly based upon a common belief in the progress of the whole. (Cheers.)

Mr. Harcourt

Mr. HARCOURT, in seconding the resolution, said that for more than nine months his office had been the clearing house of the patriotism and the generosity of the Empire. (Cheers.) It had been the switch-room of messages of devotion and sacrifice and a coherer of divers races to a universal determination. The reason for all this was not only Imperial interest and Imperial sentiment, but a passionate appreciation of British methods of Imperial rule. At the end of this war he believed it would be said, and truly said, that Germany had not fought in vain, for she would have consolidated—the British Empire. (Loud cheers.)

INDIA'S MONETARY CONTRIBUTION

Finance Member's Acknowledgment

At a conference with the Karachi Chamber of Commerce on October 14, 1916, Sir William Meyer said in reply to the remarks of its Chairmen.

Lastly coming to your remarks about an Indian National War Loan I must in the first place entirely dissent from the statement that India has made no direct monetary contribution towards the cost of carrying on the war. We have made a very considerable contribution by defraying the normal cost of the large Indian expeditionary forces that have beensent to fight the battles of the Empire in various continents. It must be remembered that while we still pay for these troops we have for the time no lien on their services which would be very valuable to us in the present situation. I said in my Budget speech that we should probably contribute 7 million during 1914-15 and 1915-16 to the Home Government in this way. And as a matter of fact I think we shall probably give more. As I said too in my speech on the final Budget debate, India has contributed things far mose valuable than money: 2,000,000 trained soldiers and vast supplies of munitions of war of all kinds.

India's Part in the War

I have no sympathy, therefore, with one who belittles the part that India is taking in the present conflict. The specific suggestion that India should raise a large national war loan on which she would presumably pay the interest is one on which I could not look with any favour. A considerable amount of money has already been contributed by individuals in India to the last home war loan and no doubt the next one will call forth similar contributions. But to start a special Indian loan in India is quite a different matter. In making suggestions of this sort, it seems to me that you do not realise the gravity of the present financial situation. Here we have had in order to help to preserve the resources of the United Kingdom for war loans at home to curtail materially the borrowing programme in England which we looked forward to carriying out this year and it is not likely that we shall be able to raise any money by borrowing in London in 1916-17. As you are aware our programme of productive works have hitherto depended very largely on borrowings in the London market. We have now to look to India for such money as we can borrow and consequently those programmes will have to be very largely curtailed. The lending capacities of India are, as experience has shown, still very limited. I need only remind you in this matter of the complete recent failure of the Rangoon Port Trust to raise a loan of 7 lakhs at 4 per cent. And we cannot face the prospect of depriving ourselves of the aid which we shall have to look for from them by letting them be diverted to a Home war-loan. I may also remind you that the present finacial year is estimated to close with a heavy deficit and with the prospect of the war continuing in 1916-17 the same is likely to occur. Then this makes it still more impossible to act in the way you suggest. Believe me, gentlemen, the first duty of those who, like yourselves, have thrown in their lot with India, is to India and I would ask you to use your superfluous cash in subscribing to the Indian Government loans. India, as I have already pointed out, has materially helped the Empire in this crisis. The best way in which she can render further help is to be prosperous and contended internally and to rely as far as possible on her own resources financially. But although I differ from you materially on the proposal you have put forward it is a matter of great satisfaction to me to think from the spirit that animates your address that whatever sacrifices the Indian Government may hereafter have to call upon you to bear, whether this be in the way of increased taxation or by the drastic retrenchment of expenditure in which you are intrested you will suffer them willingly, nay cheerfully for the sake of India and of the Empire of which she forms a great part.

THE INDIAN PRINCES AND PEOPLES AND THE WAR

Statement by the Secretary of State

In reply to a question by Sir John Jardine in the House of Commnos on October 20, 1915, Mr. Chamberlain madethe following statement as regards the contibutions to the war made by chiefs and princes of India:—

A very bulky and detailed statement of the offers of service in connexion with the War made by Ruling Chiefs and important persons and associations in India has been received from the Government of India, and copies have been placed in the Library. The statement includes the offers and gifts that were enumerated in the telegram which the Under Secretary of State read to the House on September 9 last year, and which has since been presented to Parliament; but even the most monumental of these have since been largely increased. It is impossible to summarise these additions, which still continue to be received as the progress of the War has given fresh opportunities of service; but the House will, perhaps, permit me to quote one or two examples to illustrate the spirit that animates the whole of India. Besides the Chiefs mentioned last year, the rulers of Nawanagar, Rajkot, Baria, Jamkhandi, Akalkot, Savanur, Barwani, Loharu, and Wankaner have been permitted to go an active service in one or other of the spheres of operations. In addition to the Imperial Service troops originally selected from among those offered, contingents from the following States have also been accepted for service in India or abroad:—Junagadh, Khairpur, Nawanagar, Bhavnagar, Janjira, Tehri, Bahawalpur, Maler Kotla, Sirmur, Bhopal, and Idar.

Three hospital ships, equipped and maintained from unofficial sources, have left the shores of India:—The "Loyalty," given jointly by a number of Ruling Chiefs; the "Madras" given by the Madras War Fund; and the "Bengali," given by the people of Bengal. The last was, most unfortunately, wrecked on its way to the Persian Gulf; the first two have been continuously employed this year in carrying sick and wounded between India and the theartes of war.

The Nizam of Hyderabad has offered 60 lakhs for the expenses of one of his Imperial Service regiments, which has gone to the front, and of the Cavalry Regiment of the Indian Army of which he is honorary colonel. The Maharaja of Mysore, besides the 50 lakhs he had already given, has offered the services of his State in many other practical ways. The Maharaja Sindia of Gwalior, whose health has prevented him from going to the front, has made further munificent gifts in money and in kind, including a motor ambulance fleet and six armoured aeroplanes. The Begum of Bhopal, in addition to large contributions to relief funds and other services, has sent 500 Korans for sick and wounded Moslem soldiers. The Gaekwar of Baroda gave 5 lakhs of rupees for the purchase of aeroplanes. The Maharajas of Kashmir and Patiala and the Jam of Nawanagar, besides other services, are jointly maintaining a hospital for officers in a house at Stanines, which his Highness the Jam has given for the purpose.

It is not possible to enumerate the offers and the contributions of various kinds that have been received from individuals and from associations in British India. It must suffice to say that they demonstrate the firm determination of all classes and creeds to take their place in fulfilling all the positive duties of citizenship.

Nor have the notabilities and tribes of the borderland been behind the inhabitants of British India in the spontaneity of their expressions of loyalty. The offers of service by the Frontier Militias, the proposal of the Khyber tribes to furnish an armed contingent, and the subscription by the Wazirs of Bannu of their allowances for one month to the Relief Fund, are striking examples. Beyond the border, the Chiefs of Baluchistan made valuable offers of camels, and the Sheikhs of Koweit and Bahrein contributed to charitable funds in India. The Maharaja of Bhutan, besides offering the financial and military resources of his State, contributed a lakh of rupees to the Relief Fund. The Prime Minister of Nepal added largely to the munificent gifts mentioned last year, and has rendered his Majesty's Government most valuable services by the military facilities which he has accorded. The Dalai Lama of Tibet, as was stated last year, offered 1,000 soldiers at the outbreak of war ; his continued sympathy with the cause of the Allies is shown by the fact that on hearing of General Botha's victories in South-West Africa he ordered flags to be hoisted on the hills around Lhassa, and spcial prayers to be offered for further victories. It will not perhaps be out of place in this connexion if I add that his Majesty's Government have received striking proofs of the friendship of the, Amir of Afghanistan and of his determined loyalty to the British alliance.

It has not been possible for the Government to avail themselves of all these many and varied offers of service, but our appreciation of them is not less on that account. And the House will agree with me in seeing in them conclusive evidence of the unshaken solidarity of the princes and peoples of India and of the neighbouring countries, without distinction of race or religion in defence of the vital interests of the Empire. (Loud cheers.)

INDIA AND THE WAR

Mr. Chamberlain's Tribute

The Secretary of State for India issued for publication the following statement, which, in view of reports of unrest in India which were circulated abroad, and especially in America, was made by him to the American Press.

The Internal Situation

Statements, says Mr. Chamberlain, are often made that India is on the brink of revolution, and before the war there was much talk of sedition. There were also seditious acts, culminating in an attack on the Viceroy. The wish being father to the thought, Germany eagerly swallowed all such stories, and jumped to the conclusion that when Great Britain was involved in a life-and-death struggle with a European power India would seize the opportunity to throw off British authority. In this expectation the Germans used every means to turn the situation to their own advantage and create trouble for us.

At one time there was a small amount of trouble, but how trifling was the result as compared with the hopes and expectations of the enemy ! Out of a population of 320,000,000 there are naturally some who are discontented, and even a few who are violently inimical to Government.

Missionaries of Sedition

A body of malcontents did start a conspiracy to overthrow British rule. The plot originated among the Hindu settlers in California, who, for a year or two before the war, had been carrying on an anti-British propaganda. Soon after the outbreak of the war a number of these sailed for India with the design of seducing Indian troops and starting a concerted rising which was to have taken place in February, 1915. They had been led to expect to find India in revolution. As a fact, they found it quite tranquil, and all the leading men enthusiastically supporting the

British Government. So far from raising the Punjab, as they hoped, the missionaries of sedition met with a stubborn resistance from the villagers whom they approached, their attempts to seduce troops failed, and they did not secure the adhesion of a single man of any influence and importance.

The complete failure of their fantastic conspiracy is the best evidence of the stability of British rule. In Bengal, too, there has been a series of daring outrages in the shape of murders and robberies which have produced some alarm. The ignorance and credulity of young men have been taken advantage of. Facts have been mirsrepresented to them, and they have been led to believe that India is oppressed and that expulsion of the foreigner will bring the millennium. And some of these young men of the student class have committed crimes of violence, which are, however, condemned by all influential Bengalis.

These are the chief instances of trouble we have had in India since the war began. They are trivial when viewed in comparison with the whole situation. Apart from them the state of India is perfectly satisfactory, and now, after twenty months of war, the Viceroy is able to report that "the internal situation could hardly be more favourable."

Splendid Loyalty and Substantial Help

India, instead of being a cause of anxiety, has been a substantial help to the Empire in time of need. She was able to send troops to aid in the great battle of Ypres in those critical days when the Germans were striving to reach Calais. She has also sent troops to Egypt, Gallipoli, East Africa, Mesopotamia, Persia and China. No fewer than twenty-one regiments of Indian cavalry and eighty-six battalions of Indian infantry, in addition to the troops placed at the disposal of the Government by the rulers of the Indian Native States, have been fighting the battles of the Empire far beyond the Indian borders. These have been despatched completely equipped, and, in addition, drafts more than filling up the vacancies caused by casualties have been regularly forwarded. And the people of India, sepoys and Maharajas, villagers and highly educated public men, have given their support because they are deeply convinced that in this war the British Empire is fighting in a just and righteous cause. The Indian people have a high sense of right and wrong. They saw that in this war the Allies were in the right, and they regarded tha cause of the Allies as the cause of India.

The Rally of The Princes

In fact, the rally of India to the Empire has been one of the most remarkable events in its history. Directly the war broke out the rulers of the Indian Native States took the lead in asserting their enthusiastic loyalty to the King-Emperor. Numbering nearly 700 altogether, they with one accord rallied to the defence of the Empire and offered their personal services and the resources of their States. Among the many princes and nobles who volunteered for service in the war was the veteran Sir Pertab Singh, who, in spite of his seventy years, refused to be denied the right of serving the King Emperor in Person, and who spent many months in the trenches in Flanders. Twenty-seven of the large States which maintain Properly trained and equipped troops for Imperial service placed these at the disposal of the Government. Other chiefs offered large sums of money. Three States offered camels and drivers. One chief in addition to his troops, offered his private jewellery. Large contributions were made to the patriotic funds. Outside India altogether, the Nepal Government placed the whole of their military resources at the disposal of the British Government, and the Dalai Lama of Tibet offered 1,000 troops and stated that innumerable Lamas all over Tibet were offering up prayers for the success of the British arms.

—And of the People

The Viceroy received thousadds of telegrams and letters, from every quarter expressing loyalty and the desire to assist. They came from every community, from all manner of different associations, religious add political, from all the different creeds and from countless numbers of individuals, offering their resources and their personal services. In the Viceroy's Council one of the Indian members moved a resolution, which was carried unanimously, declaring that the members of the Council, voicing the feeling that animated the whole of the people of India, desired to give expression to their feelings of unswerving loyalty and enthusiastic devotion to their King-Emperor, and an assurance of their unflinching support to the British Government. This resolution further expressed the opinion that the people of India, in addition to the military assistance now being offered by India to the Emperor, would wish to share in the heavy financial burden imposed by the war on the United Kingdom, and thus to demonstrate the unity of India with the Empire.

Material Aid

During the progress of the war further offers of help have been and continue to be received, and more of the chiefs have been able to serve at the front.

Three hospital ships, equipped and maintained from unofficial sources, left the shores of India—the "Loyalty," given jointly by a number of Ruling Chiefs; the "Madras," given by the Madras War Fund; and the "Bengali," given by the people of Bengal. The Maharaja of Mysore offered 50 lakhs of rupees (£ 333,000) to the Viceroy for any purpose in connexion wlth the war to which the Government decided to devote it. Similarly, the Nizam of Hyderabad, the premier Chief in India, offered 60 lakhs of rupess(£ 400,000) for the expenses of one of his regiments which has gone to the front. The Maharaja Sindia presented a motor-ambulance fleet and six armoured aeroplanes. Other chiefs made further contributions to patriotic funds. And from beyond the borders of India came additional proofs of support. The Chiefs of Koweit and Bahrein, on the Persian Gulf, contributed to charitable funds in India. The Dalai Lama of Tibet, on hearing of General Botha's victories in South-West Africa, ordered flages to be hoisted on the hills round Lhasa; while the Amir of Afghanistan gave striking proofs of his friendship and of his determined loyalty to the British alliance.

The Congress and Public Opinion

The leading Indians in the provinces directy administered by the Brish Government were equally decisive in their expression of loyalty. And last December the distinguished Bengali president of the Indian National Congress, Sir S. P. Sinha, said in his opening address: " The supreme feeling which arises in our minds is one of deep admiration for the self-imposed burden which England is bearing in the struggle for liberty and freedom, and a feeling of profound pride that India has not fallen behind the other portions of the British Empire, but has stood shoulder to shoulder with them by the side of the Imperial Mother in her sorest trial."

The Indian National Congress is an independent unofficial body. In ordinary times it is higly critical of the Government. The expression by its president, and the resolulion of loyalty wihch was passed, may be taken as representative of the feeling of the great bulk of the Indian people. (*May 12, 1916.*)

UNWRITTEN HISTORY

Lord Hardinge on India and the War

Lord Hardinge, in the course of a conversation with the London correspondent of the " New York Times, " gave the following account of Indian affairs since the outbreak of the war :—

For months during the early period of the war India was practically denuded of British troops, and the Indian contingent who went abroad to fight the British Empire's battles amounted to some twenty times the total of the force which was sent to China. It the time of the Boxer rebellion.

The Policy of " Mutual Trust "

" How was this possible ? " Lord Hardinge was asked.

" Only because of mutual trust," he replied. " At the outset of the war I had consultations with the leaders throughout india. I frankly expcsed to them the situation and the needs of the Empire, and was assured that there would be no serious trouble an India. I believed their assurances, and my trust has been amply justified. "

We sent out of the country no less than 300,000 men to various fields of the Imperial battle-line in France, Egypt, China, Mesopotamia, East Africa, Gallipoli, and even the Cameroons. These consisted of both Indian and British troops. When it is remembered that the British Army of occupation usually numbers some 73,000 men, and that at one time for a few weeks there remained only a handful of British troops—something between 10,000 and 15,000 men—in a country with a population of over 315,000,000, one can realise that such a course of action would have been foolhardy in the extreme had there been any real foundation for the report of widespread and serious disaffection spread from enemy sources. If India had been as disloyal as the Germans would doubtless have liked it to be, our policy would have been tantamount to an evacuation, with the probability that we were condemning the few thousand of troops left behind, practically without artillery, and the whole white civilian population to being submerged under a tidal wave of revolt. This situation was, however, purely temporary, for since the period of the first few months of war the garrison of India has been considerably reinforced by Territorial and garrison battalions and Territorial artillery.

The Indian Empire gave to the British Empire, in the critical early stages of the war, when England's resources in artillery were, as is well known, entirely inadequate to the needs of the situation the whole of its artillery of the most modern and up-to-date pattern, with the exception of a few batteries, which were kept on the north-western frontier for protection against attack from without. And even these batteries were reduced from six to four guns. India also supplied the British Government with great quantities of shells, rifles, and small arms ammunition, and the Government of South Africa with shot and shell.

From these facts it is apparent that the Indian Government had full confidence in the loyalty of the Indian princes, chiefs, and peoples. How has that trust been justified ? A few striking examples will prove more than generalisations about India's loyalty.

Plots that Failed

In the winter of 1914–15, about 7,000 Sikhs returned to India from the western part of the United States and Canada. They were imbued with revolutionary ideas, aud were, doubtless, under the impression that the whole country was ready to rise. They made their way up country, and, arrived in the Punjab, committed all sorts of excesses, not stopping at murder. This was in February, 1915. Not only did they fail to subvert the population, but when the Government took in hand the task of suppressing the disorders and hunting down the perpetrators, they were invariably assisted by the Sikh peasants, who in numberless cases themselves seized and handed over the guilty parties to the authorities.

In the Punjab these returned Sikhs were undoubtedly parties to a conspiracy which had for its object to cause a general rising and seize in the first instance the Ferozepore arsenal. It was through the unfailing loyalty of the people themselves to the British Raj that the conspiracy came to naught.

There is ample evidence that German assistance, financial and otherwise, has been given to agitators. One plot was directly instigated by Germany through various agents, who were supplied with considerable funds. This was an ambitious scheme—nothing less than to create a general revolt, which was timed to break out on Christmas Day, 1915. However, the Government was furnished with full information of the projected rising, and was able to forestall it, and render all preparations abortive. The centre of this plot was in Bengal, where there has always been a certain amount of anarchist activrity. Another specific instance of the loyalty of the people in presence of a conspiracy of this kind occurred in Balasore. Here the presence of a number of revolutionaries was signalised to the police by villagers, whom the agitators had approached. The peasants themselves assisted the police in tracking down and arresting the revolutionaries some of them actually giving their lives in their loyalty to the Government in a mêlée that occurred when their arrest was effected. Yet again, in every case where attempts were made to suborn sepoys of Indian regiments from their allegiance information was given to the Government by the soldiers themselves.

Crazy Revolutionaries

Of course, there is a certain amount, though small comparatively, of disaffection and disloyalty in India. Among a population of over 300 millions, comprising so many varieties of race and sect, and representing all degrees of political and educational development, how could it be otherwise? But even so, this discontent is anarchistic rather than revolutionary. It has no constructive programme. It represents a desire to tear down authority, not a plan to set up a new authority. I wish to state most emphatically—and American readers can take my word for this—that the persons at the back of this movement—such as it is—are not the intellectuals of India—they are to be found among the half-educated. The Ghadr party, so called because of the paper of that name, which is printed abroad and introduced secretly, is frankly anarchistic. It is encouraged by a few crazy people in the United States and Western Canada, and probably subventioned by Germany. The head of the Ghadr party is Hardyal, who was at the time employed at the German War Ministry, and who was last heard of, I believe, in Japan. This anarchistic party is small in numbers and influence, but it is desperate and dangerous. Its gratest strength lies in Bengal. Its predominant plan is to reduce the province to chaos by the murder of police and officials. As you may remember, the last Viceroy was, like other individuals before him, the victim of these methods. I am happy to say I am quite recovered from the wounds I received on that occasion, and that my Indian servant, who was on the elephant with my wife and myself, has also quite recovered. It may interest people to know that it has been proved that the bomb was thrown by one of a gang of three, of whom two have already suffered capital punishment for other crimes of a similar nature.

Controversies Suspended

Since the outbreak of the war all political controversies concerning India have been suspended by the educated and political classes, with the object of not increasing the difficulties of the Government's task. In certain cases, where drastic legislation was necessary, the Government was able to pass it without the lightest opposition in the Imperial Legislative Council, which consists of sixty-eight members, with an Indian representation of about thirty, and a Government majority of only four. Speeches made by Indian members of the Council are striking testimony to their sense of increased responsibility. There is no doubt of the very considerable political progress of India. Even during the five and a half years of my stay there I noticed a vast political development. Those politicians whose ultimate aspiration is self-government have become more moderate and sensible in their demands as they came to realise that it was impossible for India to stand alone. It is unquestionable that this improvement is an outcome of the reformation of the Councils undertaken by Lord Morley and Lord Minto.

The Princes and the People

Nothing could possibly exceed the loyalty of the Indian princes and chiefs, who have shown themselves ready to make great sacrifices for the sake of the Empire. They have contributed enormous sums of money and large numbers of Imperial service troops employed both abroad and in India, where in some cases they are fulfilling the service of British regulars. Most of the princes and chiefs offered themselves for service with the British colours, and many of them are actually serving. There has not been one single instance of even disaffection or even of absence of patriotism on the part of the princes or chiefs, whom I regard as the pillars of the State.

No doubt there was a good deal of perturbation on the littoral of India during the ravages of the "Emden" in Indian waters, but the people of India now realise the immunity they enjoy from the predominance of British sea-power. There are certain Germans in Persia and in Afghanistan—in the latter country they are now intered—who had wireless stations at Ispahan—now in the hands of the Russians—and at Shiraz, and transmitted all sorts of information, true and false.

The North-West Frontier

This doubtless accounts for some of the reports which have been current in America, particularly with regard to conditions on the North-West Frontier. It is true that during the past year we had no less than seven very severe attacks from tribesmen just outside our frontier. They were, however, all repulsed, and the tribesmen severely punished. Frontier disturbances now present a very much more serious problem for the tribesmen, in view of the introduction of aeroplanes, armoured cars, and high explosives. No serious trouble need be apprehended.

At the outbreak of the war, his Majesty the Amir gave the Viceroy the most solemn assurances, which have since been renewed, of his intention to preserve the neutrality of his country; and I, as the ex-Viceroy, have the firmest confidence, in spite of the very great pressure put upon him by certain members of his family and some prominent officials, encouraged by Germans and Turks who are in Cabul at the present time, and who went there with letters from the Kaiser in the hope of inducing the Amir to proclaim a Jehad on the North-West Frontier, that his Majesty's promises will be loyally performed. In Tibet the Dalai Lama is most loyal. We heard that Lhassa was beflagged after General Botha's successes in South Africa.

INDIA'S SERVICES TO THE WAR

Statement by the Viceroy

In his opening addess in the Imperial Legislative Council at Simla on September 5, 1916, Lord Chelmsford made the following summary statement of what India had done during the past two years:—

The winter of 1914–15 was one of the most critical periods of the war for it was evident that the troops then available on the Continent and in the United Kingdom were inadequate for the defensive role allotted to them and that the only way, pending the raising and training of new Armies, in which the position could be saved was by replacing the Regulars serving in the Mediterranean and Colonial garrisons, with Territorials and by drawing upon India for troops to the fullest possible extent. The demands then made on us were honoured in full and with the utmost promptitude. Two cavalry and two infantry divisions, completely equipped in every respect with staffs, horses, transport ambulances and all requisite auxiliary services were despatched to France. Of the endurance and gallantry displayed by the Indian Corps, while serving in the trenches during the trying winter of 1914–15 and again in the severe fighting that took place in the following spring I need hardly speak, for its details are known to you all. Despite a wastage in *Personnel* of over 150 per cent. per annum and a considerable loss in animals the Indian Corps were always kept up to strength and liberally provided with clothing, munitions and equipment from India.

At the same time as the despatch of troops to France, nearly the equivalent of a Division was sent to East Africa while one Cavalry and six Infantry Brigades were despatched to Egypt Very soon after, a Division complete in every respect was sen. to Mesopotamia where it has since been largely reinforced while smaller forces were employed at Muskat in the Persian Gulf and at Aden. All these forces were based on India which provided the drafts of men and animals and the food, forage and material required for their maintenance.

Besides the heavy burden of having to meet the needs of Expeditionary Forces at the same time, India had to maintain the troops on her frontiers and to conduct operations which attracted little attention at the time but which were nevertheless on a considerable scale.

A Great Imperial Asset

The Army in India has thus proved a great Imperial asset and in weighing the value of India's contribution to war, it should be remembered that Indian forces were no hasty improvisation but were an Army being fully equipped and supplied which had previously cost India annually a large sum to maintain.

I wish that time would permit of my giving you an account in greater detail of the assistance in men and material which India has furnished and is furnishing to the cause of the Empire. It would show the strain that is still imposed upon us by the maintenance of these large forces overseas. It would not, however, be justifiable at this stage of my speech to inflict on you a full recital of these facts and figures. Still I cannot refrain from mentioning a few salient points.

On the outbreak of war, of the 4,598 British officers on the Indian establishment, 530 who were at Home on leave were detaind by the War Office for Service in Europe. 2,600 combatant officers have been withdrawn from India since the beginning of the War, excluding those who proceeded on service with their batteries or regiments. In order to make good these deficiencies and provide for War wastage, the Indian Army Reserve of Officers was expandad from a total of 40 at which it stood on the 1st of August, 1914, to one of 2,000.

The establishments of Indian units have not only been kept up to strength but have been considerably increased. There has been an augmentation of 20 per cent. in the Cavalry and of 40 per cent. in the Infantry, while the number of recruits enlisted since the beginning of the War is greater than the entire strength of the Indian Army, as it existed on the 1st August 1914. These remarkable results may be attributed to the confidence inspired by the British officers of the Indian Army, the cordial co-operation of the civil authorities and the loyal response of the people of India.

Recruiting has been opened to several classes to whom military service was previously closed. Considerable public interest has been aroused by the sanction given for the formation of a Bengali Double Company which will be trained on the frontier and sent on active service. The Bengal Stationary Hospital recently broken up rendered admirable service in Mesopotamia and its record there was one of which the promoters of the scheme may well be proud.

Military Transport

The despatch of so many Expeditionary Forces from India has necessitated a great expansion in military transport. Four Camel Transport Corps and twenty-seven Mule Corps have been despatched on service representing a total of over 13,000 men and 17,000 animals. To replace these units and provide for wastage, some sixteen new transport corps and cadres have been formed.

Six labour corps have been sent to the front and some 1,500 overseers, draftsmen, clerks, storekeepers, carpenters, smiths, mechanics, etc., have been despatched to Mesopotamia for duty on military works and India has supplied large stocks of military material.

Medical Personnel and Equipment

In respect of medical *personnel* and equipment, and this is a matter in regard to which the Government of India have come in for special criticism, India's contribution towards the overseas expeditions have been on a very big scale. Forty field ambulances six clearing Hospitals, 35 Stationary Hospitals, 18 General Hospitals, 9 X-Ray sections, 8 Sanitary sections, 7 advanced Depots and 1 General Medical Store Depot are now serving overs as The *personnel* provided for these units and other services amounts to 258 officers of the R. A. M. C. 704. I. M. S. officers, 40 lady nurses, 475 Assistant Surgeons, 845 Sub Assistant Surgeons, 734 British Nursing orderlies, 284 Indian ranks and nearly 20,000 Indian followers. In order to meet the demands on the Indian Medical Service 344 officers have been withdrawn from the Civil Service employment and some 200 private practitioners and Civil Assistant Surgeons have been given temporary Commissions. In the subordinate branches 206 Assistant Surgeons and 560 Sub-Assistant Surgeons in various kinds of civil employment have been released for military duty. The strain which has been caused to the Civil Medical Departments by these changes and withdrawals has been very great. In the medical sphere, in fact, it must be patent to all that in responding to the demands made upon it, we have gone as far as it was possible to go.

Ordnance Department

The efficient working of the Indian Ordnance Department is shown in the enormous increase in the output from our factories and arsenals since the outbreak of war. To name one item only I note that we have supplied the War Office with stores to the value of a million sterling, includiug some 265,000 high explosive empty shells manufactured by the Munitions Branch. The Indian Ordnance was only organised to supply the requirements of military operations of the North West Frontier and it is, therefore, no small tribute to its power of expansion that it has been able to deal so successfully with such vastly increased demands.

Royal Indian Marine

The work of the Royal Indian Marine in connection with the war has been of great importance. 171 vessels have been chartered and fitted up as transports and since the beginning of the war the sailings of transports from Bombay alone had up to the end of July, numbered 926 and the arrivals 1,044. These figures give some idea of the shipping and transport work which has to be dealt with by the marine and embarkation staffs at Bombay Moreover 70 steamers, 100 launches and 207 lighters and barges have been purchased and prepared for service in Mesopotamia. 192 officers and 7,000 Indian seamen and stokers are now serving in the Government Flotilla on the rivers of Mesopotamia. The work has been carried on under high pressure in the Royal Indian Marine dockyards and repair shops for river craft have been established in Mesopotomia.

Railway Service

The Railway Board, besides controlling the manufacture of munitions outside Ordnance factories, has provided the material and *personnel* required for the construction and working of military railways in East Africa, Mesopotamia and at Aden.

In addition to all the material, rolling stock and engines required for these Railways, the Board has equipped and staffed a number of workshops overseas and constructed, on behalf of the military authorities, various descriptions of vehicles and equipment such as armoured motor cars, motor lorry bodies, water tanks, as also eleven complete armoured trains and 7 hospital trains.

Hon'ble Members will, I think, agree that the account of what India has contributed towards the war is a record of loyal achievement of which, as the Secretary of State recently stated in Parliament, she may indeed be proud.

Assistance from the Ruling Princes.

The Ruling Princes and Chiefs of India have continued to give invaluable assistance towards the prosecution of the war and the relief of sick and wounded soldiers. Among receni contributions have beeu the Rajputana gift of over 4½ lakhs for aircraft machine guns and motor ambulances, the gift of Rs. 45,000 by His Highness the Maharaja of Rewa and the Solankt Rajput Chiefs for the purchase of aeroplanes, the gift of one lakh of rupees by His Highness the Maharaja Holker of Indore and of Rs. 22 lakhs by His Highness the Maharaja of Bikaner from his privy purse. Hospital accommodation has been provided or offered by their Highnesses the Maharajas of Patiala, Bikaner Datia, Benares, Jind and Kapurthala the Maharao of Sirohi, the Nawab of Malerkotla and the Raja of Suket and substantial contributions have been received from the Rulers of Cutch, Limbdi, Dasada, Snopur, Bahawalpur, Faridkot, Manipur, Dhar, Jaora. Barwani, Ali Rajpr, Raghugarh ann Shahpura.

The Imperial Service troops are still doing very valuable work on the various fronts, notably the Mysore Lancers and the Bikaner Camel Corps in Egypt, the Kashmir Rifles the Jind Infantry and Faridkot Sappers in East Africa and the Malerkotla Sappers in Mesopotamia and I am glad to hear that the Kashmir and Jind Durbars have recently received a special message on congratulations from General Smuts on the efficiency of their troops. The Sirmur Sappers had the distinction of assisting in the gallant defence of Kut.

The veteran warrior, His Highness Sir Pratab Singh, after a brief visit to India has returned to France where, with His Highness the Raja of Rutlam, he continues to uphold the name of he Rajputs far patriotism and valour.

To all these and to those other rulers whose princely gifts and loyal services have been acknowledged on previous occasions, I should like to offer, on behalf of myself and my colleegues in this Council, our warmest and most sincere thanks.

A FILM OF INDIAN WARRIORS

Mr. Chamberlain on their prowess

A new series of war pictures was shown for the first time, of September 11, at the West End Cinema Theatre, Coventry Street. They were taken on the Western front by Mr. H. D. Girdwood, geographer and historical photographer to the Government of India, and deal almost exclusively with the Indian Expeditionary Force. The performance was held under the patronage of Queen Alexandra, and among those present were Viscount French, Sir Sam Hughes, Sir Thomas Holderness, Sir James Dunlop Smith, General Sir C. C. Egerton, Lieutenant-Colonel Sir Francis Younghusband, and Mr. and Mrs. Austen Chamberlain.

Mr. Chamberlain, who was introduced by Mr. G. F. Sexton, proprietor of the West End Cinema, made a short speech before the pictures were thrown on the screen. He said that, though they met in the heart of London, the occasion was really an Indian occasion. The pictures had been taken in France under circumstances of considerable difficulty, and at a time when the censorship of all efforts either a literary or pictorial representation of the doings of our troops was more strict than in recent times. Nothing could be more remarkable than the way in which, at the call of the King-Emperor, the Government, the princes, the people of India had responded with all they had to offer, and had contributed, and continued to contribute, to the successful prosecution of the war.

The scenes photographed took place in Erance, and there were Indian troops in France to this day, but it was uot in France alone that-the Indian Army had helped to maintain the honour of the flag. On the battlefields of France they had won recognition, but in East Africa, in Mesopotamia, at Aden, in Gallipoli, in Egypt, and in all the theatres of war Indian troops had borne their part with credit to themselves and with advantage to the Empire. In that audience there might be among the convalescents whom he saw before him men who had served alongside these Indian troops and who would be glad to bear testimony to their gallantry, their endurance, their patience, and their perseverance in circumstances which were new, strange, and alien to anything they had hitherto experienced.

While in men and in material the Indian authorities had nobly come to the assistance of the Empire as a whole, they had had their own cares and dangers to foresee and meet, and especially he had in mind the occasion when they repelled a serious rising in our own territory. No one could think of Indian co-operation in-this war, no one could speak of it, without thinking of the forces in Mesopotamia, reinforced largely, but still consisting in the majority of the troops sent from India. We had all sympathised with the hardships they had undergone; we had all admired the heroic efforts they made for the relief of their comrades at Kut. We shared the disappointment that, owing to the difficulties of climate, communications, and floods, the troops failed to achieve the object they had in view. He thought that sometimes Mesopotamia bulked too largely in the public eye as the Indian contribution to this struggle. No one would understand the responsibility which the Government and the military authorities had undertaken, no one would understand the contribution India had made to the defence of our common interests, unless they understood that the effort in Mesopotamia, great as it had been, was but one of many undertakings in which her troops had borne a glorious share.

Perhaps he might be permitted to speak of the fellowship established between comrades in arms, established, for instance, between the famous Anzac Corps and the Indian soldiers who fought with them. He hoped that with such results as these the war might arouse throughout the whole Empire a keener interest in the country which had given te us so largely and so readily, might secure for Indian aspirations new sympathy in all parts of the King-Emperor's Dominions, and might result in a closer union, not merely among peoples of our own blood within the Empire, but among all the peoples whose fate was being decided by this great struggle, whose liberties, whose honour, and whose peace were at stake, and who in the measure of their ability were contributing in men and in material resources to secure our common success.

At the close of Mr. Chamberlain's speech, Mr. Sexton called for three cheers for India, and Mr. Girdwood gave an account of his experiences in securing the pictures.

The Pictures Described

"With the Empire's Fighters" is the title given to the film. The pictures were taken, as Mr. Chamberlain said, under circumstances of great difficulty and danger. Mr. Girdwood followed the Indians into the front trenches and even beyond, getting a machine-gun bullet upon one occasion through his camera and having other very sharp escapes while he was about it. Regarding these doings, eighteen months and more ago, the Censor at the time allowed us to learn nothing, and Mr. Girdwood must have been considerably the earliest in the field of authorised kinematographers. He obtained some of his best pictures by climbing into a tree with his camera and daring the German sniper to do his worst, which he very nearly did.

The cavalry come first upon the scene The Jodhpur Lancers are seen going into action, and Jacob's Horse moving up to support an offensive. We are taken right into the front-line trenches, eighty yards from the German lines, and watch Sir James Willcocks examining machine-gun emplacements manned by Dogras and Indian cavalry, while the continual fall of leaves across the picture tells of the German rifle fire overhead. Glimpses are given of the Prince of Wales at his chateau in France; and Sir Pratap Singh, the Maharaja of Barwani, and other Indian princes ride across the screen. Sikhs are shown chanting hymns outside a French farmhouse, Gurkhas playing football with some of our Highlanders, Indian cavalry tent-pegging and trick-riding, and Jats wrestling. Another picture represents perhaps the strangest sight of all: Gurkha pipers marching up and down and playing the "Marseillaise" before a crowd of French peasants. The post-office in the field and the admirable arrangements made for the wounded also form part of the record.

The sight in the Somme film of two English soldiers being shot down as they climb out of the trench has aroused discussion whether these things are not too terrible to be filmed, but long ago Mr. Girdwood was photographing far more ghastly things, such as a rush by the Gurkhas over a German trench and across it to storm the second line. The cutting ef the German trench is visible in the foreground, and the little men with the cocked hats come running across by the hundred. They seem to be lying down to take cover when scores and scores of them fall down in the brushwood. The reality is far grimmer; these are the dead and wounded. Nothing can give a better idea of what the taking of a trench means than this picture, with the Gurkhas swarming into the captured trench and consolidating it, while in the background the Red Cross men are carrying the dead and wounded away.

Terrible and lacerating as this section is, and a similar one which shows the storming of a trench by the Leicesters (who formed part of the Bareilly Brigade), the film is well worth seeing, and we hope that arrangements for its exhibition in India have not been forgotten by the India Office.